W9-BGD-711

WHEN SEA BILLOWS ROLL

Paul T. Schlener

Phil. 1:6

1/28/16

PAUL SCHLENER

ASPEN
HIGHLANDS
PUBLISHING

"Beautiful Books. Powerful Words."

www.AspenHighlandsPublishing.com

Graphics by Dan Nuckols
www.HighlandsGraphics.com

Printed by White Birch Press, Spooner, WI

ISBN: 978-0-9816328-1-0

For ordering, see www.WhenSeaBillowsRoll.com.

Military photos are courtesy of the Naval Historical
Center and the National Archives. Other photos are from
the personal collection of Paul Schlener

Scripture taken from the
HOLY BIBLE, NEW INTERNATIONAL VERSION.

Copyright 1973, 1978, 1984 International Bible Society.
Used by permission of Zondervan Bible Publishers.

Excerpts from Streams in the Desert, published 1954,
Cowman Publications, Mrs. Chas. E. Cowman

DEDICATION

This little book has been written especially for, and dedicated to the offspring and future descendents of John and Fran Schlener, Paul and Jessie Schlener, and all of Jessie's brothers and sisters, and Damon and Ruth Nuckols. No matter what your family names might be by the time you read these simple sentences, our prayer to God is that you already have—or will—realize that you are a sinner, and that you must come to know the Lord Jesus Christ as your personal Savior. He came down from heaven, to shed His blood on a cross in payment for my sins and yours, so that we sinners might be forgiven and saved for eternity by faith in Jesus Christ as personal Savior. Think it over and make the decision soon.

ACKNOWLEDGMENTS

Ten hard copies of When Sea Billows Roll, were sent to various friends and relatives to read with a request to criticize, holding no punches. I thank them for the long hours they spent looking for discrepancies as they poured over the pages. I was greatly helped with good suggestions and encouragement to publish it.

Miss Kristen Stagg, graduate of Kent University, Ohio, published author of four books, and widely experienced editor, graciously consented to edit this book, When Sea Billows Roll. She did a noteworthy edit of my book, Port of Two Brothers, published in June 2000.

I wondered how Kristen could possibly find time to work on this manuscript together with long drives to work, plus trips to and from the hospital while caring for her mother who suffered for months in agonizing pain until she went to her home in heaven. But Kristen persevered and finished her excellent work on When Sea Billows Roll. Thank you, Kristen.

Mrs. Rose Reynoldson, East Wenatchee, Washington, retired Composition professor at Seattle Pacific University, took extra time to fill the margins and blank spaces taking copious notes with excellent suggestions, and encouraging remarks. I am thankful for Rose's input, and for her husband Elmer who no doubt was forced to more kitchen activities in the process. You folks have been a great encouragement to us for many years.

Dr. J. Don Jennings, published author with decades of serving the Lord, is widely acclaimed and highly honored as a Bible teacher and preacher (www.drdonjennings.com). He took time to read the raw manuscript, When Sea Billows Roll, and made important suggestions that helped smooth out some of the rough parts. Thank you, Dr. Jennings.

Thanks to nephew Phillip Schlener, retired Airforce Leutenant Colonel, now missionary to Portugal who offered some suggestions that I appropriated. I am encouraged to know that the other three of John's and Fran's family John, David, and Allene Hopson, have encouraged me to write this book which is dedicated to them.

Mrs. Laura Grenier, an avid reader and teacher, graduate of Cornerstone University, Grand Rapids, Michigan, agreed to review this story. As Pastor's wife of First Baptist Church in Moses Lake, Washington, and a super busy church secretary for a number of years, she helped me reword various sentences while finding typos which she typed on separate sheets, making it easier for the ancient author to copy. Thank you, Laura.

While recuperating in the Life Care Center of Ritzville, Washington from the results of a head-on collision on highway I-90, two of God's dedicated servants from Richland, Washington, came to my rescue. Unable to put weight on either leg, I struggled to do some writing in a loose leaf notebook until Bob and Denise Morse appeared in the doorway of my room with a laptop computer for me to use. You can guess what a blessing that was, after I finally got the hang of using it. Thank you, Bob and Denise for that favor, and for all the years of encouragement you have rendered to Jessie and me.

Paul L. Schlener
August, 2010
Moses Lake, Washington

FORWORD

While penning these paragraphs about my experience on board the great ship USS CAPE ESPERANCE, I thought of my shipmates and other sailors who served on board the good ship since the Cobra and Viper typhoons. Threatened by onslaughts of wild wind and pounding water, none of us on board realized what a seaworthy chunk of steel was holding us up. Hearing eerie sounds from steel bending, twisting, snapping, and to watch airplanes being swept across the flight deck and into the sea plagued us with fear. Sudden thrusts of the entire ship by megatons of water made us wonder why this top-heavy rig didn't capsize. Through the most powerful storm on record she showed her stuff, giving ship's company reason to thank God, and the shipyard workers who glued her together.

Some of my shipmates didn't have a birds-eye view of what was happening above decks as did the few of us who were stationed on open bridge. Below decks the main concern was to cling to something ... beams, pipes or stanchions to avoid being slammed onto the steel deck or tossed against bulkheads. What else could be accomplished?

I'm sure that every sailor on board during those violent hours has different stories to tell about the storm, and will see things in my paragraphs that differ from their experiences. I've read every book I can find by navy officers, and quotes from enlisted men who served on board the CAPE ESPERANCE and other ships during the battles with wind and waves. I found that some of their opinions, descriptions, and measurements are not synonymous with each other. This is to be expected. It would be well for my readers to jot down their own experiences while serving on board our ship as memoirs to leave with their family and friends.

Paul L. Schlener

1

A grueling cattle car ride on the Great Northern Railroad
was the first of many to naval training stations along the
route from North Idaho to Astoria, Oregon. It gave opportunity for young sailors, some of whom had never left
home before, to feast their eyes on snowcapped Rocky
Mountains and peer into the depths of yawning canyons.
Many of us had never seen the Pacific Ocean before. "Join
the Navy and see the world" we were told. Jim and I were
on our way.

"Jim, can you believe how they herded us into these ancient rattletrap trains? It's kinda like we're white-faced
Herefords. I'd heard talk of 'cattle cars' before; now I know
how they got that name!"

I was talking to a fellow Seaman Second Class, Jim
Sweeney. We'd just completed boot camp at Farragut Naval
Training Station in North Idaho, and were lowly apprentice
seamen in the United States Navy with nary a glimpse of
saltwater to show for our training thus far. Our infinitesimal

promotion permitted us another white stripe on our cuffs and a bigger one around our right shoulders. It was nowhere near the distinction of gold braid, but it didn't take much for us "swab jockeys" (the Navy's own nickname for its sea-based personnel) to feel cocky.

Jim responded to my comment, "Yeah. The way the chief petty officer yelled at us, I wondered why he didn't save his breath and just use an electric prod like the cowpokes do at auction sales back in Iowa."

Jim didn't have anything to brag about. Although he didn't have a mean hair on his blond head, the well-proportioned rugged farm boy was used to foul-mouthed talk and toughened to hard work. But his walk and speech were equally slow. Platoon leaders screamed at him to "get the lead out" of his feet.

It bothered me when Jim made the mistake of going on a one-day liberty with the wrong group of boys who took great satisfaction in getting him stupidly drunk. Jim lost control of most of his faculties, leaping off a moving bus and in the process breaking his arm and scraping his face. Scars still stood out fresh on his face from that ill-judged escapade.

We stood among a crowd of boot camp survivors like us, waiting to be transferred to who-knew-where, although most of us didn't care. The guys dawdled around, smoking endless packs of cigarettes while waiting for a yeoman to tack the next list of assignments to the bulletin board. We had lived through fevers with aching muscles, thanks to immunizations; and numbed toes from marches in the bitter cold on the frozen ground of an arena the size of a football field known as "the grinder" without benefit of long johns. Athletic hot bloods reluctantly learned to accept saliva-laden insults hurled by mean-spirited superiors in nose-to-nose confrontations— without reciprocating.

Crowded in front of the bulletin board, nearly crushing the humble yeoman with his papers and thumbtacks, we jostled one another as we searched for our names. Jim and I, along with a trainload of others, found our names listed under the heading "CVE Pool". A tall, lanky kid who might have been a swimmer, piped, "What the heck kind of pool is *that*?"

On tiptoe next to me, Stanley Odenbaugh from one of the other Farragut boot camps was barely tall enough to qualify for military service. His body made up in muscle tone what it lacked in height. You wanted to be on Stanley's side in the event of a showdown on land or sea.

Stanley's broad smile revealed a shiny gold crown as he spoke up, "I got word from a friend who is already in the Pool. He says CVE stands for Carrier Vessel Escort. Looks like we're doomed to become galley slaves on a 'baby flat-top.' They also call them 'Kaiser's coffins'. He says they sink like empty tomato cans when they fill up with water. But there are so dang many of 'em, the Navy doesn't care because they're still making 'em by the dozen."

Jim shrugged his shoulders, drawling, "I dunno. Maybe your friend is right. Whatever it means, we can't turn back now. Gotta take what we got. We asked for it. Nobody forced us to join up."

In this case, CVE pool meant a group of sailors available for the single purpose of filling Admiral Halsey's tiny aircraft carriers with sailors for Task Force 38. Admiral William F. "Bull" Halsey was commander of the U.S. Third Fleet, consisting of 132 ships, in the Pacific Ocean. According to biographers, the admiral's nickname and facial ex-

Paul Schlener, age 17

3

pressions were equally descriptive of the man's character.

When General Douglas MacArthur vacated the Philippine Islands ahead of invading Japanese forces, it fell to the Third Fleet to man a vast concentration of aircraft carriers that filled the skies with planes raining non-stop strikes on enemy vessels and island strongholds. We sailors of the CVE Pool would eventually learn of the existence of a natural enemy more fierce and powerful than the Japanese imperial armed forces.

* * *

But our destination on this train ride was additional instruction before being assigned to a Third Fleet ship: gunnery training and fire fighting. The naval instructors had no trouble maintaining discipline, for boot camp had built raw recruits up to optimal health, while simultaneously melting us down to opinion-less nubbins of "Yes, sir", "No, sir" and "Aye, aye, sir".

The instructor at firearms training announced, "Hey, guys, you're looking tough after getting ground down on 'the grinder'." His statement elicited a wave of laughter. Sinewy, suntanned, and sporting a perpetual furrow between his brows, he reminded me of a Montana rancher: a good shot.

He told us, "We can have a heck of a good time here with these lethal weapons *if* you do *exactly* as I tell you and show you. *If* you do not obey instructions, there's a whale of a chance that you will be sent home to your mom and dad in an oblong box."

Rifle and pistol practice left all of us recruits with sore hands and shoulders, not to mention ringing ears, but none of us got out of line during gunnery training. It was a good thing boot camp preceded these particular training classes, because otherwise serious accidents would undoubtedly have occurred, thanks to young know-it-alls. I am convinced that Navy philosophy in boot camp is: "You do not know anything. Therefore, in order to survive your stint in the Navy, you will learn to do everything the Navy way."

It was actually fun shooting 20mm anti-aircraft guns with tracer bullets at target sleeves made from light cloth and towed by airplanes. The tow-plane pilots were either very young and fearless, or nervous wrecks, knowing that a trigger-happy recruit might set off his dozen rounds at the plane instead of the sleeve.

My group lucked out with our fire-fighting instructor. His simple sentences carried impetus from the first moment he addressed us. "Men [none of us had ever been called that before, and our chests puffed out in pride], I'm supposed to teach you how to put out fires like those that ignite after a torpedo or bomb hits your ship. A fanatic kamikaze pilot is just waiting for the order to plow into your ship a heck of a long way from shore and you guys are the fire extinguishers."

He had our full attention. Few of us ever imagined having to put out a fire on an all-steel ship, or worried about being bombed. Our instructor's stocky face sported scanty eyebrows.

"Looks like he's been singed from showing how to do it too often," I wise-cracked out of the corner of my mouth to the guy standing next to me.

"It isn't easy to put out a fire when burning petroleum is the culprit," our instructor continued. "I won't threaten you, but I strongly suggest you do exactly as I tell you and show you. If you do, you have a better chance to avoid becoming broiled sausages, just like I haven't, so far. . . ."

Each of us sailors had to take turns being first in line to face the roaring inferno of scorching flames, fiercely gripping the heavy brass nozzle of a water hose. The nozzle man was motivated to do everything right in double-quick time before he lost his eyebrows. The rest of us cowered behind him, clinging to the thick water hose, trembling with fear at the incredible heat and knowing our turn at the nozzle would come far too soon. This experience made me wonder about hell. I had heard it described as a whole lake of fire, but always figured hell was just another swear word from the lengthy lists accumulated by the saltiest sailors.

* * *

Once fire training was complete, we prospective sailors were loaded once more into cattle cars for one last ride. The cars ground to a halt at a platform where military buses, painted a flat grey color, waited for us. The Navy driver at the wheel sported a funny grin. He knew what we had been through and what still lay ahead. A smooth bus ride through town helped us forget the monotonous clickety-clack of the cattle cars. Our mouths watered as we passed grocery stores, restaurants, and an ice cream parlor.

The driver stopped, pulled a lever that opened the door, and admitted a wide-eyed Chief Petty Officer. Stiff as a hickory stick, the C.P.O. clutched a clipboard, announcing, "You have arrived in Astoria, Oregon, where the Columbia River empties into the Pacific Ocean. Follow me to board the *USS Cape Esperance, CVE 88*, to which you are assigned for duty."

Like chickens released from a crowded coop, we newbies poured out of the buses hard on the heels of the petty officer. Tied up at the pier was an enormous grey box with a super-sized 88 painted on its tower. The USS Cape Esperance was an odd looking ship: drab grey with a snub nose, its rear end sawed off square. The huge wooden top, flat as a dining room table, held a forward tower on the starboard side with nothing else to dress it up. The tower stuck out past the edge of the hull, making it appear lopsided. How could an airplane land on what must look to be the size of a postage stamp from a few thousand feet up? Anti-aircraft guns mounted along a narrow catwalk stood ready just below the flight deck. Ah, yes! The firearms I recognized, now well aware as to their intended purpose.

CVE 88 USS Cape Esperance

A shrill whistle over the public address system repeated a tune twice, followed by a bass voice that carried clear across the Great Divide. "Now hear this! Now hear this! All hands on deck for muster."

There was no welcoming committee or brass band to strike up the Navy hymn to meet us. Instead, officers shouted orders that separated the mass of sailors into divisions. Several of my buddies from boot camp were assigned with me to the Second Division.

Another triple-shrill from the P.A. system introduced the same bass voice from the boatswain. "All hands below decks! Secure all personal gear in assigned lockers, and report to hangar deck in thirty minutes!"

Once we completed those orders and returned to the hangar deck as instructed, the PA bellowed again with less-thrilling news. "All hands turn to! Embark all supplies from dock to storage areas!"

Some of the not-so-robust sailors responded by hunting out hiding places to rest. Their mistake was rewarded with, "Get off your rear ends, you goldbrick landlubbers, and stiffen up to the best attention your lazy bones can muster." They leaped to their feet, stomped out their cigarettes, and froze at attention.

Quietly, humbly, the boatswain started to lecture. "I'm the boatswain in charge of loading this ship with supplies before we shove off for a shakedown cruise. I'm in trouble if it doesn't get done on time." Then with face crimson in anger, he bellowed, "The brig is still nice and new just waiting to make shirkers of duty like you birds comfortable for a few days on bread and water. I simply ain't gonna let you jerks get me in trouble. If you do, I'll arrange some unlovely extra duty that will make you wish you were back in Sunday School Class. Now, get the heck to work!"

The next morning after chow, the PA again summoned us sailors to the hangar deck where scanty decorations heralded some sort of celebration. The official commissioning ceremony for the *U.S.S. Cape Esperance* was already in progress when we arrived on the scene. Either I hadn't listened carefully or hadn't read the notices, because I was surprised to see about a hundred civilians milling around our hangar deck. The Navy had invited parents and friends of the Esperance's sailors to attend the ship's commissioning. Many of my friends waved to people they recognized and looked forward to talking with after the ceremony.

"See anybody you know, Jim?" I asked my buddy.

"Naw," he answered. "My folks are already plowing, getting ready to plant corn."

I didn't bother searching for familiar faces, but took advantage of the offered refreshments. Not only was I ignorant of the commissioning ceremony taking place, even had I known in advance, I also knew that Dad struggled twelve hours a day with his business and couldn't take time off, while Mom babysat and did nursing. She had been dead-set against Dad signing the documents that permitted me to drop out of high school and join the Navy at seventeen years of age, so it's not likely she would've wanted to attend the ceremony either.

Standing at "parade rest," we sailors suffered through a dreary reading of the list of our ship's officers. Our captain, Robert W. Backius, and Commander McDonald delivered lackluster speeches on the subject "*Esperance* action." The time for refreshments and mingling with guests provided a welcome respite.

"Hey, Schlener, there's ol' Stanley lugging a big black case," Jim said, pointing out our friend. "They probably stuck him in the Third Division."

"Well, if it ain't Mr. Colorado himself," I exclaimed, thumping Stanley on the back. "Man, I thought you were AWOL and skeedadled back to Pike's Peak when you heard we were shipping out."

"Not this swab jockey!" Stanley retorted. "I'm in for the whole hog or nuthin.'"

"What ya got in that suitcase? Looks out of place among all these sea bags," Jim said.

Stanley explained, "It's my squeeze box; my wrinkle machine. They said I could bring it on board."

"That's fantastic," I yelped. "We can hold jam sessions if you'll let me beat on the case with my drum sti—"

I never finished my sentence. Standing not ten feet away from me was my mom, listening and smiling. I swept her into a hug before introducing her to my buddies.

"How on earth did you get here, Mom? I had no idea! I didn't even know invitations were sent out." I peppered

9

Mom with comments and questions, careful with my language. I'd had my mouth swabbed out with soap as a kid, and badly needed another treatment now, if Mom only knew!

She said, "I just finished taking care of an invalid lady and was able to buy a round-trip bus ticket for the commissioning. I just had to see my sailor boy once more before he went to sea!"

Mom was away from home a lot when she babysat or nursed ailing folk. I thought of Dad's extended work schedule, sometimes twelve hours straight, and often without a cook when Mom was trying to make ends meet during the Depression. Dad wasn't grief-stricken when Mom was away for a while. Although he missed her caresses, cooking, washing, and ironing, he took great pleasure in gutting the refrigerator, throwing away leftovers that had sprouted hairy mold.

Our time together on the ship passed too quickly. When Mom and I said our goodbyes, she held on tightly, as if afraid to let go. She thrust a small package into my hands. In a quavering voice, she said, "Dad and I want you to take this Bible with you to sea. We'll be praying for you, Little Brother," she called me by my nickname. "Be careful, won't you?"

Both of us were too choked with emotion to speak, and then she was gone. Memories of childhood and adolescence flooded my mind as I watched Mom disappear from view, down the gangplank.

2

"We have an anchor that keeps the soul
Steadfast and sure while the billows roll,
Fastened to the Rock which cannot move,
Grounded firm and deep in the Savior's love."
(We Have An Anchor, Priscilla J. Owens, 1882)

As I recalled, Mom introduced me to her friends around town as her "baby," far from amusing to a teenaged boy. A pang of sorrow hit me as I recalled how disrespectful and disobedient I had been at times. Despite my misbehavior, Mom kept me covered with clean clothes and full of good food while I attended school and worked as flunky for two grocery stores. I accumulated a shameful list of swear words from both grocery store managers. During summer vacations, I worked on farms driving teams of horses, pitching hay, mowing lawns, whatever jobs I could find.

One of the grocery store managers, a bulky six-feet-plus, sounded like a Sunday school teacher as he chatted with customers who asked to leave their purchases in the store after closing so they could finish their shopping in town.

"Why, Mrs. Garterblossom, you certainly may leave them right here. Take your time! I will personally unlock the door when you finish."

But the second he snapped the lock on the front door at closing time, he drew from an endless supply of colorful invective, cursing farmers who were late in picking up their groceries. I couldn't blame the Navy for my bad words; I'm sure I contributed as many swear words as all the other sailors.

One memory from my teenage years revolved around summer trade school in Spokane, where I learned to roll my own cigarettes from tobacco purchased in tiny cloth bags. I felt like a real man with the little tobacco trademark tag hanging out of my shirt pocket. Cigars and a yellow bowl-filtered pipe qualified me for the upper echelon of smart-aleck teenagers. I'm so thankful I had never even heard of the illegal drugs that are so destructive to today's youth.

Four of us high school buddies took off in a Model A Ford one summer, hoping to join the Forest Services disease control crew. Blister rust was one of many diseases that invaded the sap wood and inner bark of pine trees, producing external blisters from which the disease gets its name. The Forest Service hired vacationing high-schoolers, and we four intended to be among them. Our parents didn't know where we were going, but neither did we! Before skipping town, I charged a pair of expensive logging boots to my dad's account at Kreugel's Men's Store, and purchased a one-pound can of pipe tobacco before skipping town.

My sister, Ruth, 15 years older than I and a school teacher, gave me a silver dollar along with her advice: "Paul, you shouldn't go away. You shouldn't smoke yet. You're only 16 and besides, it's expensive." I thanked her for the money without admitting that I knew she was probably right.

My quartet of happy-go-lucky nitwits finally realized the old car consumed gasoline at the rate we inhaled carbohydrates. What small change we had went—literally—up in smoke. I'm embarrassed that we had the nerve to raid neighborhood gardens, cutting the garden hoses to siphon gasoline from cars parked along darkened streets. There were no locks on gas caps in those days, and we boys took advantage of equally unprotected homes to steal canned pears and peaches from unlocked cellars.

With my last 20 cents, I bought bacon grease at the back door of a restaurant in St. Mary's, so we boys could fry fish in an old pan we found half-buried in the sand under a railroad trestle. I wished I could've sold the remaining pipe tobacco in my one-pound can and the .22 rifle we used to plink gophers along Highway 95. I was tormented by visions of Mom's Sunday dinners, the leftovers in the icebox (mold and all!). It never occurred to me to let Mom and Dad know where I was or what I was doing. None of us cared in the least how our careless behavior might affect our parents.

Two of us managed to land positions with the Blue Mountain Cannery in Dayton, Washington, during pea harvest. Lawrence went to the field to pitch vines where he had intervals of rest, while I was assigned to a flatbed truck, stacking crushed, soggy pea vines as they tumbled non-stop out of the threshing machine. Two grown men quit the position the day before I took over. Although the work was too strenuous for me, I made it to the bitter end of my shift.

The sweetest silence I had ever experienced in all my sixteen years was when the menacing machine finally stopped and I jumped off the truck. My trousers hung loose, even with my belt cinched on the last hole. The spring in my steps had sprung as I dragged my body to the office to pick up my first paycheck with fingers trembling from exhaustion.

"Hang in there, kid," the boss cajoled, promising, "You'll have a partner to help you tomorrow."

Pea harvest didn't last long, but with a little money burning a hole in my pocket, I was determined to travel to Seattle and investigate the weird religion that snagged both my older brother, John, and his girlfriend, Fran. I wondered if he wore a broad-brimmed black hat and button-down shoes. I thought, *Maybe he hangs a bag of magazines on his shoulders and distributes them on street corners. Or maybe he jumps over church benches and rolls on the floor, playing with rattlesnakes while he dances.*

3

"When winds are raging o'er the upper ocean,
and billows wild contend with angry roar,
'Tis said far down beneath the wild commotion
that peaceful stillness reigneth evermore."
(Harriet Beecher Stowe, Streams in The Desert p.304)

When I was only nine, John had already turned eighteen. Even though John could be mean to me, like all older brothers with their younger siblings, I held him in high esteem. I boasted to my playmates that my big brother drives a truck for the Civilian Conservation Corps (CCC), which sounded important until I tumbled on the fact that the truck he drove was only a wheelbarrow.

When girlfriends visited lover Johnny, he paid me a nickel and threatened that I should skedaddle unless I wanted trouble. I turned blackmail into a small business, raising the price of my disappearance to a dime.

That was half a lifetime ago; now I held a cheap black

suitcase. A roll of white adhesive tape formed white letters on the side of my suitcase to spell SPOKANE. With my hair slicked back with Fitch's Brilliantine and shrugged into a spiffy sports jacket and pressed gabardine slacks, I stood nonchalantly along State Highway 124, one shiny-shoed foot perched on the suitcase as if I were totally unconcerned with whether or not I ever got a lift.

My intention was to appear non-threatening to drivers, but I was either courageous or stupid! Before leaving home, I'd made an eight-inch blackjack from oil-tanned harness leather gleaned from my dad's leather shop. Number two lead shot from three shotgun shells thickened one end of the little bludgeon, and the broadest corset stave "liberated" from my mom's lingerie (she never missed it!) gave flexibility to the handle. As I pondered the possibility of being offered a ride by some thug, the flimsy weapon wouldn't have stood a chance against a firearm of any caliber, but I was reassured by the presence of the blackjack within handy reach in my coat pocket.

In hindsight, I must've looked like Little Lord Fauntleroy or a card shark from Las Vegas. I'm not sure if it was the bravado and courage of youth or sheer stupidity on my part that made me hitch my way across the West. After riding with my mom in an old Ford as a child, I doubt I would have accepted a ride from any female driver at this stage of my life, even had one appeared. I had sat in the rumble seat of the old Ford, the better to make a quick escape if Mom should meet the disaster her driving skill indicated was a real possibility.

My first taxi driver was a hefty, rosy-cheeked farmer, driving a battered old farm truck with a front end that shimmied so bad we were all but dancing across the road. He kicked the door open and yelled, "Jump in, kid! Ain't you a heck of a way from home?" he wheezed around a curved pipe resting on his unshaven chin. I noted with nostalgia his can of Prince Albert tobacco, similar to the tin I once used for storing gopher tails. The tin fit perfectly in the pocket of my overalls.

I gave my gallant driver a rundown of the summer, ending with the admission, "Before I go back home, I want to visit Seattle and see my older brother that got religion. I'm running out of dough, so I plan on hiring on with a cherry-picking crew to make a few bucks first.

The farmer dropped me off on the highway barely five miles from where he picked me up. I made it as far as Wenatchee, thanks to the services of smooth-talking salesmen in shiny automobiles and other farmers.

On the outskirts of Spokane, I struggled to get the correct spelling for WENATCHEE on my suitcase, nearly exhausting my supply of white adhesive tape. I enjoyed excellent room and board for those few days, picking cherries and thinning apples, bolstering my depleted supply of silver dollars. I really shouldn't have been paid at all! Thinning apples supplied me with ammo to pelt at other migrant workers, while a generous portion of the cherries I picked went to satiate my own appetite.

*   *   *

Months before my bold escape from Bonners Ferry, Idaho, with my high school buddies, I had watched from the living room window at home when my brother John "got religion." At least, that's what I called it. I didn't understand what was taking place out by the car belonging to Harold Winters, a traveling salesman, who pulled into our driveway one afternoon. A friend of the family—and a friendly man—from my family's South Dakota days, Harold's waving black hair framed a face that was the picture of health.

In those days of the Great Depression, Mom, ever the hospitable hostess, did what she could to make visitors welcome. Delectable aromas aroused our digestive systems as heavily laden platters of food graced the table. One call from Mom was all we kids needed to spring from our activities and take our places at the table. And boy! Was Harold ever hungry!

"Aunt Rena," he said, both hands busy keeping the food traveling from plate to mouth, "there's nothing like a home-cooked meal after eating in greasy spoons. Thank you, thank you, thank you."

I kept out of the way, with nothing to contribute to the non-stop conversation swirling around me, and barely able to answer simple questions. After breakfast the following morning, Harold bade his farewells, saying to John, "Come out to the car with me. I have something to tell you before I leave."

I watched from the living room window as Harold reached into his car for a thick black book. I knew it was a Bible. John stood there, hands in his pockets, still sleepy after his normal late-night activities. The young salesman placed one foot on the chrome bumper of his car, rested the open Bible on his raised knee, and proceeded to talk while John focused on the ground in front of him, scraping a little dirt loose with the sole of his shoe.

At first, the salesman was all smiles. But when Harold glanced at the Bible, he grew as serious as a judge. John nodded a few times, but kept his eyes on the little mound of dirt he was making. He didn't utter a word until Harold placed the Bible in John's hands. They both looked at the pages while Harold pointed to a place on the page and motioned for John to read it. I couldn't hear a word of their conversation, but from that day on, John was different.

At the time I left home with my buddies, John was engaged to marry popular Fran Read who, with her sister Louise, was a Bonner's Ferry High School yell queen. A farmer's daughter, Fran also worked as an usherette in the local movie theatre. Fran couldn't swallow John's religion, and returned his engagement ring. Later, I overheard family conversations which revealed the fact that Fran changed her mind and became a devotee of John's religion, and eventually even took his ring back.

Months later when asked to be best man at their wedding, I couldn't believe they were serious. I had suffered through my sister Ruth's wedding in South Dakota and didn't want any part of another one! I was to wear a suit made over from one owned by the late venerable mayor of Conde, South Dakota, population 421. Skipping town with fellow carefree runaways ensured that John and Fran got hitched without the company of little brother Paul.

And now, here I was, riding a bus over Steven's Pass to John and Fran's place in Seattle, the biggest city I had ever seen. I decontaminated myself of the telltale scent of cigarette smoke by using strong soap in the filthy bus station's restroom followed by potent bay rum lotion. My breath was handled—I hoped—with a wad of chewing gum. It was a supreme sacrifice on my part to drop a nearly-full pack of king-size Wings in the trashcan.

Once the taxi deposited me on the newlyweds' apartment doorstep, I made several feints at their door. I wondered if I should scram and forget it, but finally worked up the nerve to knock for real.

I hadn't told my brother and sister-in-law I was coming, but they received me warmly—hugs and even a kiss from the yell queen. They actually seemed glad to see me!

A fancy plaque on the wall caught my eye the moment I stepped into John and Fran's living room. It proclaimed that Christ was the head of this home; John and Fran apparently wanted everyone to know who was boss. Another ornate hardwood frame let us know that "Prayer changes things." Oh boy! I was on hyper-alert for being pounced on and force-fed a mega-dose of religion after spotting those two signs.

John was old—a whopping twenty-five—to my youthful sixteen. Scant muscle on my boy's frame gained imperceptible (one might almost say, invisible) bulk from hard work. By stretching, I could make myself a tad taller than he. So we were forced to engage in a wrestling match, not just a couple of gentle, smiling grips, to test our strength against one another. We strained, rolled, and twisted while thumping the floor with our knees, elbows, and noggins. Anxious residents from the apartment below stopped our good-natured battle with a series of healthy blows to their ceiling. My big brother didn't actually pin me, but when we were forced to call a halt to the proceedings, he may have had an edge on me.

Although without much experience in the culinary arts, newly-married Fran prepared me delicious meals. At breakfast, my halved grapefruit had been carefully pre-cut, allowing each section to be easily lifted with a spoon. This was followed by perfectly fried eggs and crispy bacon. I also slept between smooth, clean-smelling sheets, thanks to Fran. But despite this attention to my creature comforts, I didn't want to stay long, fearful that John and Fran would attempt to forcibly convert me.

After touring the city, John and Fran took me to church where I met some of their friends. One of them, Paul Goodman, was a DC-4 pilot who flew the "hump" of the Himalayan range between India and Burma during World War II. One zealous church member asked me what church I attended. I responded that I had been a member of the Methodist Church since my folks had me baptized there in infancy. I figured that "baptized" would gain me the respect to halt further inquiries, but his reply astonished me. "Son, there won't be any Methodists in heaven."

Did that ever burn me to a crisp! I was ready to make sure there was one less whatever-he-was on earth that very moment. I might not make the grade into heaven—that I knew—but he had just insulted Mom and Dad by his remark, and I wanted no part of his religion. I wanted no part of him either, and kept a healthy distance from him for the remainder of my visit, certain I was doing him a favor by not taking him out of this world then and there!

The night before I left John and Fran's, we sat talking on their sofa. John nailed me with a simple question I clearly recall, more than 60 years later. "Paul, are you saved?" he asked.

I thought a couple of seconds before wise-cracking, "Well, John... are you saved?"

He surprised me by stating that he was, telling me the day he accepted Christ as Savior, and expressing joy over the event.

"Well, then, I must be saved, too," I shot back. "I admit I've been a mean rascal and have done plenty of bad things, but I haven't lived long enough to get into as much skullduggery as you have. So if you're saved, then I must be too. We have the same Mom and Dad, right? They always go to church."

4

"O Lord God Almighty, who is like you? You are mighty, O Lord, and your faithfulness surrounds you. You rule over the surging sea; when its waves mount up, you still them." Psalm 89:8-9 NIV

Sailors swarmed the dock and the decks of CVE 88, toting supplies in preparation for a cruise to Samoa like nipper ants carrying bits of foliage to their subterranean home. At muster, my assignment was delivered straight from the lieutenant with an icy stare. "Slennah [my surname always posed a challenge to my superiors], youah watch will be at the helm to and from Samo-er. You'll have foah owahs ohn, and foah owahs off, around the clock." The lieutenant's accent seemed to indicate that he was from the Northeastern United States, but wherever he hailed from, his message came through loud and clear.

"Aye, aye, sir!" I sang, as if grateful for the promise of interrupted sleep for the round-trip to Samo'er, wherever that was. I wanted to confide in the lieutenant that I get lost on my bicycle even with all kinds of landmarks and directional signs. How in the world could I navigate a giant ship in the middle of the ocean? However, boot camp taught sailors—smart alecks and humble alike—not to argue or make clever remarks, so I kept my skepticism to myself.

The first time I took the helm, my pulse accelerated like a machine gun, while my fingers trembled in their white-knuckle grip on the big wheel. I had never even driven a car, so I had no background from which to steer a five-hundred-foot ship with any hope of arriving any-where close to our intended destination. The fact that there was nothing for me to bump into helped allay some of my initial panic. Once I got the hang of it, it was actu-ally kind of fun. I was proud of the fact that I started my driving career by tooling a 500-footer around the Pacific Ocean! But after a few days, the novelty wore off and mo-notony set in. There were no mountains or buildings; no roads; no hitch-hikers to liven the scenery; just me with my feet planted in the same spot, hour after hour, keeping both compass needs in their appointed positions.

I never needed to look out on the ocean during my watch, just focus on the compasses. Full moon and stars, sunrises and sunsets were wonderful beyond description. A sparkling moonlit path on the water led all the way from our ship to the horizon. On more than one occa-sion, I daydreamed too long watching the flying fish flut-ter by and not paying attention to the compasses.

My instructor, boatswain second class Oliver, kept ex-tremely close tabs on me after a notable reprimand over the intercom. "Who is the anesthetized, cock-eyed sleepy-head on the helm?" the Skipper roared. "Why is this ship staggering as if she's intoxicated? This is no [bleep] –ing time for a zigzag course. We want to get to Samoa on a straight course, for the love of Pete!"

The Skipper's next eruption came an octave lower as he inquired with feigned patience, "Who in the devil's name is the boatswain in charge? Doesn't anyone have a hold on the wheel? Can't anybody steer this ship?!" The lower tone was scarier than the loud blast.

Boatswain Oliver, even with a wind-burned face, suddenly looked anemic. He was roundly roasted for not keeping his eye on me, the true culprit. I rejoiced to the depths of my heart that I was only 150 pounds of irresponsible shark bait, while Oliver took the fallout for my behavior.

My next watch with the same boatswain was graveyard, midnight to 4:00 a.m. Yours truly again took the wheel. Although a good guy, Oliver was obviously none too pleased at being teamed up with me again. This time, Providence saved Oliver from having to attend Exec's mast [court] with Commander McDonald.

Monotony and drowsiness somewhere around 2:00 a.m., overtake sailors on watch, especially on calm seas. The endless moan and gentle vibration from the ship's engines, combined with a smooth rocking from starboard to port and dim lighting act like mild anesthesia. For brief moments, two compasses doubled to four, as my knees buckled, startling me back to wakefulness.

Oliver handed me a flashlight, saying, "Here, Schlener. Take this and get us a thermos of coffee from the galley. Might as well snatch anything edible while you're there."

Now I was wide awake, thankful for the break. I shimmied down the exterior ladder, my flashlight waving as I clung to the metal ladder's rungs with one hand and a couple of fingers. On my return trip from the galley, I had to juggle a heavy thermos and sandwiches, making the maneuver that much more difficult and sending out even wilder arcs with my flashlight.

Arriving back at the wheelhouse eager to begin snacking, I met captain's orderly, seaman Fong, who stood waiting, his face devoid of all expression. As he spoke, I thought I detected the slightest twinge of sympathy on his face, but it was gone so quickly, I couldn't be sure of what I'd seen.

"What's your name and what division are you in?" he demanded. "The captain wants to know."

Somehow, I knew that the man with four gold braids on his sleeves, the virtual king of CVE 88, hadn't run me down to compliment my fine performance at the helm, although I couldn't imagine how he detected I'd all but fallen asleep at the wheel.

I was soundly reprimanded over the intercom for flashing a white light after dark—in a battle zone, no less!— putting the entire ship and her crew in life-threatening danger. I might as well have laid out a welcome mat for a kamikaze pilot, saying "here we are". Furthermore, I was ordered to report to Exec's mast at 1300 hours on the following day.

Exec's mast is a court hearing and sentencing of transgressors by the ship's executive officer, who in this case was Commander McDonald, second in command of the Cape Esperance. I never had occasion to speak to the commander, nor did I seek for an opportunity. I had often heard him during muster, but never once saw him smile. At a little under six feet, the commander boasted a barrel chest and the beginnings of a pot belly. His sloping shoulders were too narrow to classify him as "well built," and his arms seemed too long for his torso. His protruding blue eyes and a severe tone radiated antagonism to his audience.

I dreaded the next day's mast. At one muster, after trouble with a couple of sailors, Commander McDonald challenged the entire ship's company. "Any of you guys think you're tough? Step forward right now! I'll take on any one of you, any way you want it," he dared. No one stepped forward, although at the time I wished some of the crew members built like Greek statues and experienced boxers or wrestlers, had gone a round or two with the commander. During my two years on ship, I never met a single sailor who spoke favorably of him.

But those facts didn't help with the upcoming court. By not telling the commander that boatswain Oliver had ordered me to the galley with a flashlight to get coffee, I prevented the boatswain's being busted a rank or two lower, sentenced to time in the brig, or both. I figured I couldn't be busted any lower than I was, so why get my friend in trouble? Because we were long past the days when it was accepted custom to throw delinquent sailors overboard, my punishment was ten hours of extra duty in the engine room. Those ten hours taught me to respect the boys who spent endless days below decks in perpetual heat radiated by the ship's giant engine. And I became Oliver's new best friend in the process.

*   *   *

The deep blue waters of the South Pacific have defied description for generations. Well into my twilight years, as I sit at my desk, I can still picture that vivid aquamarine blue. All sizes and varieties of fish swam close to the ocean's surface, some jumping clear out of the water. Sharks checked out the *Cape Esperance,* but went in search of more promising prey. Squadrons of flying fish, numbering anywhere from two to a dozen, broke the water's surface in unison, their oversized fins—like wings—sparkling as they flew by. The fish can remain airborne for the equivalent of a city block before slipping back into the water.

Even these spectacular sights seemed humdrum after a few months at sea. I longed to catch sight of a rowboat, its elderly owner half-asleep under a broad-brimmed straw hat, waiting for his bobber to sink. Mental visions of rich forests, the creeks and lakes of North Idaho, my mom's home cooking, and my dad's leather shop accelerated the sluggish passage of time on watch.

The routine was soon interrupted by crossing the Equator, an event marked by something akin to the hazing that characterizes fraternities. We sailors who had never before crossed this invisible line of demarcation between the northern and southern hemispheres were considered landlubbers, not real mariners yet. Some inexperienced landlubbers actually looked for the same black line in the Ocean that they had seen on maps!

Veteran sailors who had crossed the Equator on previous journeys were known as shellbacks. Those men now eagerly dished out treatment that they'd once taken. Some of the guys spit on their hands, rubbed them together, anxious to get to work in preparing tortures guaranteed to make life miserable for us landlubbers. They could hardly wait until the boatswain piped the exact time of the crossing that signaled the commencement of the initiation.

Liquid quinine—bitter as gall—was squirted down our throats from an oil can. To refuse this beverage was a grave mistake. A target "sleeve," 30 feet long and stretched across the fantail, was filled with decomposing garbage. Each landlubber was forced to wallow through the slop while being beaten with a three-foot length of hard-packed fire hose called a shelaligh. Having lived through that, we were blindfolded then forced to kneel and kiss an overweight shellback's fat, hairy stomach smeared with hot mustard.

A cargo net, hung high above the fantail deck, was our last hurdle. All of us landlubbers had to climb up one side and down the other while being blasted from a fire hose with high pressure salt water. Those climbing to the left or right edge of the net, attempting a shortcut by swinging themselves around from the half-way mark and starting down the other side, resulted in a repeat performance of the unforgettable punishment.

Crossing the Equator Antics!

As full-fledged shellbacks, all compassion knocked out of us, we were equally cruel to the new bunch of landlubbers at our next crossing.

"Good grief! There's land sticking up from the horizon," the lookout on bridge shouted. "Slap this tub in the rump and let's get there!"

From a hazy lump on the horizon, Samoa emerged as an emerald jewel under clear blue sky. A half mile from shore, three raspy blasts from the Esperance's whistle brought a tugboat that nudged us gently to the ramshackle dock. Monkey fists, made of baseball-sized pieces of round lead, completely covered with carefully woven white cotton cord and tied to quarter-inch line, were tied to thicker line, then to heavy ropes three inches in diameter called hawsers. Once in range of the dock, at least two deck apes whirled the monkey fists and tossed them to stocky, bowlegged longshoremen, who caught them and hauled the heavy hawsers to chocks, securing the Esperance's mooring.

As our ship eased up to the dock, a brass band welcoming us to Samoa. The all-male band, bedecked in striking white, knee-length tunics, bright red turbans, and matching red sashes, snapped out marches that I once played in the Bonners Ferry High School: *Stars and Stripes Forever and Monkey Wrapped His Tail Around the Flag Pole.* Those tunes lifted us out of our mariners' misery for a while, although some of the crew were disappointed not to spy naked savages slinking through the jungle with spears or bows and arrows.

Sturdy young men sat erect in outrigger canoes, harpoons held shoulder high, taking hopeful aim at fish. Some rushed to our ship with the catch-of-the-day to extract a high price for their wares from the *Esperance's* chief cook. I chided, "Jim, you didn't even turn your head in the direction of the bronzed fishermen. Are they muscle machines or what? You should've seen that stocky guy hop out of his canoe, agile as a cat, carrying a basket loaded with fish. One of 'em, still alive, jumped out and swam away!"

"I know what you're saying, shipmate, but fishing ain't my favorite pastime. I do find it hard to let those olive-skinned Polynesian senoritas slip by unnoticed in their sarongs."

At my dubious look, he shot back, "Aw, come on, Schlener! Don't tell me you didn't notice those neat little ladies on their way to the shore, and that your interest is only in those reeking fishermen."

A few hours of shore leave released the crew from the confines of ship life. Once our sea legs wore off, we could walk without a drunken lurch. Grass and sand felt good underfoot instead of the usual steel. Intense humidity was ignored while we watched tall palm trees sway in the warm breeze and guzzled milk from the shiny coconuts dangling in bunches as far as the eye could see.

The Samoans, some of them plump with faces as round as cabbage heads, moved at a leisurely pace. Surely none of them ever suffered an ulcer or heart attack! Polynesian ladies in scanty garb were ready to charge high prices to spendthrift sailors for the grass skirts, seashell necklaces, hand-carved model outrigger canoes, and other wares made for souvenir sales.

Two plainly-dressed, middle-aged Caucasian women caught our attention as they walked briskly along the shore. Both sported long noses, light brown hair pulled back into buns, and carried books under their arms. I took them for twins, so pale compared to the local citizens, they might have just completed a shift at a flour mill.

31

Odenbaugh enlightened the rest of us clueless seamen. "With complexions like those," he stated authoritatively, "they can't be natives from any place close by. Most likely, they're what's known as 'missionaries' from some other country, trying to straighten these people out. They should come aboard ship with a few lessons for the entire crew."

I had heard the term "missionary" in Sunday school as a little boy, but this was the first time I'd ever seen one, if that's what these women truly were. I didn't know what they did, but it had to be something connected with church. I hadn't liked Sunday school one little bit as an adolescent! Forced to attend both Sunday school and church, wearing my brother John's patched hand-me-downs heartily embarrassed me. My junior boys' class was taught by a woman I thought of as elderly, wondering if she would still be living by the next Sunday. She must have been at least 40 or 50! As I reminisce, it's hard to believe that at 12 years of age, I won a Bible for one year's perfect attendance in Sunday school.

The reverends behind the pulpits were as dry as old bones. The only fun thing about church that I recalled was suppressing my hilarity at the ladies' attire, especially the plumed hats that dipped and swayed their way down the aisles, guided by sober-sided ushers. Old men who spent a week in the harvest fields under unrelenting sun and nodded off to dreamland during the service was another cause for suppressed mirth. When I couldn't contain the pressure any longer and emitted a squeak or two, my dad—arms folded, eyes straight ahead on the preacher—inserted his calloused index finger between two of my ribs as far as he could reach. Nobody saw him, but that meant show time was over for me...until the next Sunday.

5

The adverse winds blew against my life;
My little ship with grief was tossed;
My plans were gone—heart full of strife,
And all my hopes seemed to be lost.
"Then He arose" one word of peace.
"There was calm" a sweet release.

A tempest great of doubt and fear
Possessed my mind; no light was there
To guide, or make my vision clear.
Dark night! 'twas more than I could bear—
"Then He arose," I saw His face—
"There was a calm" filled with His grace.

My heart was sinking 'neath the wave
Of deepening test and raging grief;
All seemed lost, and none could save,
And nothing could bring me relief—
"Then He arose" and spoke one word,
"Then there was calm". IT IS THE LORD!
~L.S.P.(Streams in The Desert, p143}

The ship's whistle cut our tourism short in Samoa with a hiss and a squawk before settling into an agonizing moan that mirrored the emotions of every seaman ashore. Crowds gathered to see us off, Jim loathe to pull his gaze from the group of giggling young ladies who waved at us as the *Cape Esperance* backed away from the dock.

The same pep band, decked out in the finery, struck up "California, Here I Come." The words were true in this instance, for CVE 88 nosed straight to San Diego, never to return to Samoa or Astoria, Oregon, the point from which this cruise had begun.

Desperate for news from home, I answered "Here!" to every name that started with an "s" at mail call: Skinler, Sleener, Shelner, Sleneer. Dad and Mom wrote regularly, as did my sister-in-law, Fran. Each letter from my brother and his wife touched on religion and included verses from the Bible, which held little interest for me; still, I saved them in my locker.

Correspondence from Bonners Ferry was of far more interest to me. Miss Lynch, my strict high school English teacher, required her students to write letters to any of the young men who dropped out of school to join the war, an assignment that landed me a nice bundle of mail. Two of the missives were authored by attractive, baton-twirling majorettes from the high school marching band, Jessie and Cora. They twirled those shiny sticks with style, tossing them as high as the school roof. As a snare drummer, I remembered them well from when we countermarched and nearly met head-on.

Answering their letters triggered an exchange of correspondence that lasted until I visited Bonners Ferry on a ten-day leave. The bus drive from San Diego, California, to north Idaho in the 1940s was strictly for the young in good physical condition, the only qualifications I could claim at the time.

For the first day and a half, I gorged on Mom's cooking swallowing most of it whole like heels from fresh-baked bread, dripping with butter and loaded with homemade apricot jam kept me groaning in ecstasy as I recalled the slop I ate off steel trays on the Esperance.

Not being programmed for intellectual pursuits, I fine-tuned the cheap drum set in my attic bedroom and attempted to beat it to death. It required a series of ratamacues, rim shots, and paradiddles to muster up enough courage to begin my research into Jessie MacDonald's clan of Scottish descent. Jessie, the majorette, was number five of the family's eleven children.

The back porch door slammed as Mom returned from the garden, where she had fled in order to escape my loud foray into courage. A few hours of quiet would provide her some relief. I laid down the drumsticks and nerved myself up for the walk across town to check on the majorette with big brown eyes and dazzling smile.

What would happen if I took her by surprise? Who knew where Jessie might be on this lazy Sunday afternoon? Not everybody had telephones back then and time was short, so I had to take my chances. Keenly aware of my lack of natural good looks, I donned my custom-tailored and spiked bell-bottom dress blues, slathered on Mennen's Skin Bracer, and chewed a wad of gum. It took a good half hour to spit-shine my black shoes. Man, did they sparkle as I swaggered down Mahoney Hill sidewalk!

I strolled through town and across the Kootenai River Bridge to the north side of town where the MacDonalds lived. I was afraid to look at Jessie, let alone talk to her. She presented a bigger challenge than playing nozzle man at the firefighting school. The hike went by lickety-split as I struggled to rehearse carefully-worded statements that might appeal to an attractive Scottish lass.

Jessie's dad, Donald James MacDonald, and an half dozen youngsters were busy uprooting spuds in the center of their potato patch when I reached their house. Some used spades and forks, while others gathered the uprooted ones by hand, with little or no enthusiasm.

Oh, man! There was Jessie, turning up sod and pulling the spuds to one side. Even with beads of sweat dotting her upturned nose, Jessie couldn't have looked more beautiful. A combination of dark, wavy hair; a beautiful smile; big brown eyes; and a cheerful voice at a shade over five feet tall. I inhaled deeply as I glanced at her.

Caught in the midst of a humble work project didn't appear to bother Jessie. A friendly nod from her father—not much taller than the others—and a smiling "hi" from each of her siblings greatly relieved my nervous tension.

After a brief, "How 'ya doin'?" I stepped into the potato patch and relieved one of the smallest boys of his potato fork to show my stuff. I figured a humble maneuver like that might earn me a little clout with Jessie's family, a fair exchange for the utter destruction of the spit-shine on my shoes. I succeeded in getting permission to take Jessie to the Sunday matinee at the local Rex Theatre after a half hour of spud spading.

In a flash, Jessie raced to the house and underwent a complete transformation from potato digging duds to a spiffy skirt and blouse. Mr. MacDonald shoved his spade in the ground and paused to roll a fresh cigarette. As Jessie stepped from the house, he gave me a couple of sideways glances which I took to mean he wasn't pleased at the loss of a digger before the job was completed.

Donald James MacDonald, known as Jim, was thirty-two years old when he married eighteen-year-old Amelia. The young couple and their growing family worked hard to develop a sizeable homestead near Cadillac, Saskatchewan, in the mid-twenties.

Jessie recalls her dad saying, "I'm only five feet, five inches tall, lass, and I tip the scales at hundred thirty-five pounds, soaking wet." Although small in stature, Jim was recognized as one of the best teamsters in the area. In those days, that meant a man could harness and drive four or six pairs of work horses. I wondered how this lean, wiry man tossed the heavy harnesses over the big draft horses' backs, buckling them in place while controlling the friskier equines. Those powerful horses could've squashed Jim. But they leaned sleepily into their burden, obeying the pressure on their bits and heeding their teamster's familiar voice.

Jessie's uncle John, a year or two older than his brother Jim, always lived near Jim and his family, following them from one location to another. John lost his right leg at the age of 14 in an accident while on a duck hunt. He tried to kill a rattlesnake with the butt of a loaded shotgun when Bang! The poor kid took a full load of lead halfway between knee and thigh. It was eighteen miles by horse and wagon to the nearest doctor, and the lumbering animals arrived at the doctor's office barely in time to save John's life by amputating his leg.

John didn't sit on his bunk and wait for someone to take care of him. He became a well digger and carpenter; a list of requests for hammer and axe handle replacements always awaited his expert eye. Disabled though he was, John built several tiny cabins for himself. Had he made them a tad roomier, he might not have remained a bachelor until he passed away in 1967.

Little Jessie Alice was intelligent enough to take advantage of Uncle John's lost leg. She wiggled out the front gate, slipping through the space where John's missing leg would have been, and then took off full-speed knowing he couldn't catch her.

The MacDonald clan's house burned to the ground during Canada's prairie fire of 1927. Jim and Amelia took their six children, a ten-dollar bill, and boarded the Spokane International freight train, disembarking in north Idaho.

This was the family history of Jessie, the beautiful girl with whom I now anticipated watching a movie. We quickly left her house and headed downtown before her dad changed his mind and withdrew his permission.

Military personnel enjoyed prestige in those days, especially in small towns like Bonners Ferry, Idaho. "How long ya home for, sailor?" How about a piece of pie and a cup o' coffee on me?" "Thanks for being out there, son," were just a few of the comments accompanied by hearty hand shakes and back pats that made servicemen feel important.

My four-day retreat in my hometown was a boost to my morale. In addition to sleeping in my own room, crawling out of the sack whenever I felt like it, and a renewed affection from Mom and Dad gave me a sense of security and a fresh appreciation for my folks. But Jessie MacDonald, the petite Scottish waitress in the Fountain Café, remained in the forefront of my mind to such an extent that I wasn't eager to climb into a reeking, smoke-filled bus to ride back to San Diego and re-board my ship.

Minutes after boarding *Cape Esperance*, my fellow sailors and I learned that it was up to Admiral William F. (Bull) Halsey, commander of the Third Fleet, to spread a "big blue blanket" of carrier aircraft over the Philippine island of Luzon in relentless support of General Douglas MacArthur's drive to recover the Philippines from Japanese control. Halsey's blanket was provided by the enormous Third Fleet, composed of seven heavy carriers (CVs), six light carriers (CVLs), five escort carriers (CVEs), nine battleships, sixteen heavy and light cruisers, sixty destroyers, fourteen fleet oilers, three fleet tugs, and fifteen more destroyers riding herd on the oilers and baby flattops. How on earth could an array of ships that numerous, armed to the teeth with immeasurable firepower and manned with trained personnel chomping at the bit for battle, ever be destroyed? So vast was the area occupied by the Third Fleet, only a portion could be seen from the *Cape Esperance's* island, located a full sixty-two feet above the water line.

As a baby flattop, it was the *Esperance's* job to catapult fresh Navy fighter pilots into the battle zone, and take on the planes that needed repairs. We were loaded to capacity with Hellcats, Wildcats, Corsairs, dive bombers, torpedo bombers, and the ammunition and bombs these aircraft carried.

As the Japanese were being whipped by U.S. forces, they turned to the drastic option of suicide. Suicide in Japan was more prevalent in the twentieth century than deaths caused by traffic accidents. It was considered honorable. Young Japanese pilots in their late teens and early twenties were brainwashed regarding their responsibility to bring glory not only to Japan but to the Shinto religion, the Emperor, and to their own families.

These young men were allowed to decide whether or not they wanted to volunteer for a *kamikaze* flight. The *kamikaze* (trans: divine wind) was a trained pilot who flew his plane, loaded with explosives, directly into an enemy target, preferably a naval vessel. Aircraft carriers of any size were prized targets for *kamikaze* attack. Not only would a hit result in the loss of a multi-million dollar ship, but also thousands of men were lost—burned, crushed, or drowned—and dozens of aircraft destroyed. Japanese warlords thought that fearless demonstrations of suicide attacks against the Americans would psychologically weaken them and intimidate them sufficiently to lose their purpose in continuing the war.

The war became more difficult with the Allied Forces gaining ground, so more *kamikaze* pilots were needed. Their training was accelerated so that the pilot was taught to fly with limited navigation ability and no skill in landing or dog fights in the air. Poor accuracy and inferior aircraft engines caused *kamikaze* tactics to inflict more damage to the Japanese Air Force than it did on the Allies.

Aircraft carriers fully loaded with planes presented a prime target for the *kamikaze* (suicide) pilots of the Japanese Imperial Army to demonstrate their fanatic dedication to Shinto, the religion of Japan that included deities of natural forces and the Emperor, who was said to be a descendent of the sun goddess and was considered a god in his own right.

*   *   *

Numerous trips across the wide Pacific Ocean did not take the *Esperance* and her crew to centers of civilization. Beautiful Hawaii was still traumatized from the Japanese attack on Pearl Harbor; Waikiki Beach, littered with barbed wire, was no fun. The Solomon Islands weren't noteworthy. Lukewarm water surrounding the Admiralty Islands teemed with brightly colored starfish, easy to pick up in the shallow water. They felt like they were made of stone. Before going ashore, we sailors were warned not to bring back any starfish. Of course hundreds of the forbidden critters were sneaked aboard and stowed away. By the third day at sea, no one could figure out where the offensive stench originated. The unbearable odor, distributed through the ventilation system came from starfish that were so well concealed that some remained hidden until decomposition was complete.

One special highlight was Bob Hope and his troupe of Hollywood singers and dancers who entertained literally thousands of military personnel. What a boon to the vast throng of sailors, sick of the same ole', same ole'. Bob knew just what to say to make us roar with laughter. Some of the crowd of military personnel hadn't seen a female in six or eight months. And the beautiful, talented ladies in Bob's troupe were the "pick of the choosin.' Try to imagine the whistles that pierced the air!

He knew what bugged us and was masterful at joking about our problems without fear of being reported. For most of us, there was no such thing as a joke that was too off-colored. But Bob kept jokes amazingly clean. Like "What an island! You guys aren't defending this place, are you? Let 'em take it; it will serve 'em right." He greeted us, "Hello, fellow tourists! . . .Although I'm very happy to be here, I'm leaving as soon as we finish. . . . Gosh, it's hot here! I took one look at a pup tent, and it was panting. But the guys out there are really tough. They don't bother manicuring. They just stick their hands under a rock and let the cobras bite off the cuticles." He even knew that our food was served on shingles. I've never forgotten his performance and how much he did to boost our morale.

And then it was back to the same ole', same ole'. The only good part was that I was getting to see parts of the world I had only read about or seen pictures of in *National Geographic*. Without benefit of a tour guide or travel brochures, we sailors stepped onto strange beaches and shores, hardly knowing where we were. The short, muscular inhabitants of New Guinea with their dyed red hair looked dangerous to me. And of course, we cocky American sailors made fun of everything and everybody that didn't rise to our lofty expectations.

Few New Hebrideans mustered the courage to approach where we sailors swam. Poorly dressed and undernourished, they smiled unceasingly. From ten yards away you couldn't see a single tooth because their teeth were blackened by chewing betel nuts. No taverns with cold beer stood anywhere in sight; no hamburger stands, theatres, automobiles or airplanes; in short, zilch, zero, nada, that was anything like home in this strange world we were exploring.

*   *   *

"Heave around and trice up all loose gear! We are approaching heavy weather. All hands, man your assigned stations!" The news blaring over the *Esperance's* PA system wasn't good. This was the roughest weather we had encountered since the ship's commissioning months earlier. Experienced sailors evidenced concern, but greenhorn deck hands—like me—were too ignorant to worry. Blasts of wind ripped frothy peaks off high waves and carried them away, while the *Esperance* listed like never before and dozens of sailors lost their cookies.

Fortunately, the *Esperance* was positioned on the outskirts of the main typhoon, so the force of the storm didn't last long, simply left the seas rough with choppy waves. Permission to return to decks was piped over the PA too soon. Eldon, a frail, quiet kid, suffered what surely turned out to be the greatest trauma of his life mere seconds after he stepped out onto the fantail. A freak wave leaped up just as the *Esperance* listed moderately to starboard, flooding the deck with two feet of water. The volume of water receded as the ship held to the list, dragging a horrified Eldon through the guardrail chains and out to sea some ten yards from the ship. Several of us stood on deck, safe from the water's reach and stunned by this sudden turn of events. Before anyone had time to call, "Man overboard!," another wave miraculously deposited the wild-eyed, gasping Eldon right back on deck. He grabbed a chock the size of a large tree stump, hugging it with all his strength.

If I hadn't witnessed the incredible sight myself, I never would've believed such a feat was possible! "Let loose, Eldon. You're okay now," I assured my friend in little more than a whisper. Frankly, I was more than a bit shaky at the knees myself. "Let's go below and get a shot of torpedo juice (whiskey) or a cuppa mud (coffee)."

But the speechless kid refused to let go of his stranglehold on the chock. Several of us had to pry the poor kid loose, one finger at a time, and straighten his legs before we could lead him below decks to his bunk. Stanley strapped on his accordion and squeezed out "Home On The Range" and "When It's Springtime In The Rockies" in an effort to calm the petrified sailor's nerves. Eldon would rather have been in either place—a ranch or the Rocky Mountains—than in the middle of the deep blue sea. It took days for Eldon to return to normal; all that time, he hardly made a peep and his eyes carried an unusual glaze.

Years later, I read of three documented occasions of men being swept overboard by freak waves and deposited back on deck. One man, after a few minutes in the water, was deposited back on the ship's deck. Another sailor washed over the side was immediately returned onto his freighter by another wave, similar to what happened to Eldon. The third documented case involved a sailor who was washed back a full thirty minutes after being swept off the ship, while his rescuers madly searched for what they half-expected to be his remains.

Eldon's close encounter certainly gave me plenty to

think about in terms of the uncertainty of life, as if sailing the seas in the middle of a war with suicidal enemy pilots just hoping to blow us out of the water weren't enough food for thought!

6

They are HIS billows, whether they go o'er us,
Hiding His face in smothering spray and foam;
Or smooth and sparkling, spread a path before us,
And to our haven bear us safely home.

They are HIS billows, whether for our succor
He walks across them, stilling all our fear;
Or to our cry there comes no aid nor answer,
And in the lonely silence none is near.

They are HIS billows, whether we are toiling
Through tempest-driven waves that never cease,
While deep to deep with loud clamor is calling;
Or at His word they hush themselves in peace.

They are HIS billows, whether He divides them,
Making us walk dry shod where seas had flowed;
Or lets tumultuous breakers surge about us,
Rushing unchecked across our only road.

They are HIS billows, and He brings us through them;
So He has promised, so His love will do.
Keeping and leading, guiding and upholding,
To His sure harbor, He will bring us through.

Annie Johnson Flint (Streams in The Desert,p27)

During maneuvers with the Third Fleet, home port for the *Esperance* was the island of Guam. We sailors, in our attempts at fun, blistered our hides during frenzied games of baseball, volleyball, football, and basketball, drinking warm beer and even warmer purified water (we called it "putrified") from canvas bags. Yuck! After a couple of hours on this diet, some of the would-be athletes grew too wobbly to make baskets or catch passes.

Here on this island in the South Pacific, the Navy swapped battle damaged planes (duds) for the new ones we had brought from the states. We then transported the duds back to the U.S. for repair. Quick as "scat," we off-loaded the damaged planes in the USA, re-loaded with fresh ones, and headed back out to sea with the good aircraft headed for destinations known only to the radio operators and ship's officers.

About half-way to wherever we were going, with nothing to see but sky and water, a destroyer appeared about a mile off the *Esperance's* stern, gaining rapidly on our ship. Rough water indicated we were well into the South China Sea, notoriously rough sailing for about three-fourths of the year. Another irksome boatswain's pipe alerted us to the broadcast command, "All first and second divisions on weather deck. Prepare to take on pilots."

Although the *Esperance* hadn't reduced speed, the destroyer overtook us as though we were tied to a telephone pole. It pulled up about ten yards from us, and throttled back in order to keep proper distance. Glad for the change from monotonous watch schedules, we sailors darted around, cussing and laughing before we took our positions.

A quarter-inch line (roughly the size of a clothes line) called a messenger line and tied to a steel spike was fired from a special gun from one ship to another. The messenger line was quickly tied to a one-inch line, which was then secured to an enormous three-inch-thick hawser on the receiving ship's deck.

The *Esperance's* loud speaker blasted twice, "Destroyer 350 stand by for messenger line." The destroyer's crew immediately scrambled for hiding places, safely away from the spike being fired from the Esperance. In a few seconds, our boatswain hollered, "Fire!" BOOM! The steel spike shot out of our gun, carrying the messenger line over the top of the "tin can" into the water on the other side of the destroyer.

Cape *Esperance* sailors eased the lines away as the "tin can" boys pulled them over to their ship. Thick, heavy hawsers are hard to handle whether flaked out on deck, or passed from ship to dock or ship to ship. Stretching between ships, the hawsers proved strong enough to prevent the two ships from drifting too far apart. The struggle to avoid the ships smacking into one another in rough water kept both ships' helmsmen goggle-eyed, focused on the hawser's tension. If "calm seas never make good sailors," the South China Sea was perfect water for training in seamanship!

Being young at heart and in body is essential for carrier-based Navy and Marine pilots. Escort carriers like the *Esperance* presented the most difficulty for pilots. Not only is a 500-foot ship hard to locate—particularly in bad weather—it's also challenging to land on what looks to be the size of a postage stamp from a few thousand feet up. Pilots had to guess how quickly and how high the little carrier would rise or fall in swells while simultaneously throttling back to drop the plane's tail hook on the cable that kept it from continuing off the edge of the deck and into the water. The smaller the carrier, the harder to judge the rise and fall of the stern, or the pitch from starboard to port side. There was no room for "scaredy-cats" or foolhardy risk-takers at the controls of a carrier plane.

Bringing these pilots on board our carrier from a bouncing destroyer was an equally hazardous venture. Each man sat in a breeches buoy, which looked like a large version of the baby's jumper that hangs on springs from a door frame. A pilot's buoy suspends, instead, from four vertical lines from where he sits to a pulley on a guideline two feet above his head.

"Heave around and take up slack! Here comes a fly boy!" a megaphone from the destroyer barked to the *Esperance*. Deck hands on both ships tightened the guidelines to the tension of a harp string, while others pulled on the line attached to the pilot's buoy pulley.

Rough weather makes a difficult job that much harder. It's impossible for two ships of vastly differing size to maintain an even keel while cruising close together. Therefore, one pilot in his "baby jumper" might roll uphill slowly across the menacing water and step out of his breeches buoy at ease, laughing all the while; while the next pilot might speed downhill and have to be caught by the *Esperance's* deck hands before slamming onto the carrier. More often than not, a wave shoved the lighter destroyer too close to the carrier, allowing no time for the crew to take up slack in the lines before the pilot was dunked into the water. Fear of getting squashed between the ships must've crossed many a pilot's mind, several feet below the water's surface.

Then, in a panicked over-correction, the men pulled the buoy line too taut too quickly, so the pilot popped out of the water like a cork, flung up higher than his guide-line. Those with any breath left after such an experience cursed the swab jockeys for attempting to drown them! Having survived a hazardous ship-to-ship crossing, the valiant pilots were usually glad to step onto the good ship *Cape Esperance* and wolf down some chow before climbing into clean, dry airplanes. It always perplexed me how men so brave when flying thousands of feet high with little more than thin sheets of metal between themselves and crushed lungs, could be so frightened by a little water.

Still, the rough weather that day on the China Sea made taking off from the *Esperance* a dangerous feat. An aviator who makes a slight, unavoidable dip off the end of a flight deck wants to avoid this occurring simultaneously with a dip of the ship's bow so his aircraft isn't hit by the foamy crest of a big wave. On the Esperance's first trip into the battle zone, this happened to one pilot who nimbly sprang from his cockpit, unscathed, and was hoisted back aboard the *Esperance* seconds before his Hellcat disappeared into the ocean's depths.

But this day's transfer of personnel went off without a hitch, and the pilots made their way safely off the *Esperance* and out into the fray.

*   *   *

After six months at sea, the monotony of daily life shortened what little patience we young sailors had to begin with. We never saw women, children, or elderly people; only men of the same approximate age. We ate the same food and kept to the same routine day after day after endless day. After a while, it just got boring. Some of the fellows stupidly wished for an attack by enemy planes just to break the monotony. Fights over the most trivial incidents left shipmates with bloody noses, swollen lips, black eyes, and a heavy dose of despondency. Endless games of cards or dominoes quickly palled. Why bother writing letters that couldn't be mailed for who knows how long? The ship had been sanitized from stem to stern, as it had been so thoroughly cleaned.

Fire drills woke us up for an hour or so, and practice surprise attacks by U.S. fighter planes from other ships that scared us witless helped vary the pace of life at sea. Absurd past times were invented by desperate sailors. After morning clean up, a dozen guys would stand on the fan tail, pretending to troll for sword fish. Lines tied on thick swab handles plunged deep into the water as if hooked to swordfish. Didn't take much to entertain some of us!

One morning while "deep sea fishing" was at its zenith, Shockley, a prankster at heart, leaped onto the five-inch gun mount close to where the rest of us trolled for swordfish. He popped a cigarette in his mouth and called us to attention. "Fella citizens, salty sailahs, and shahk bait of the good ship *USS Cape Esperance*, lend me yer attention for a minute."

He shoved his cap to the back of his head and pulled a few curls down on his forehead while taking a long drag on his cigarette and drawing the smoke deep into his lungs before continuing. "I don't think you brave sea farahs have noticed that there ain't no boids in da sky right heah." As though controlled by a remote, we all looked up. Sure enough, not a bird in sight from horizon to horizon.

"And da wahtah is too calm foah lack o wind. Youse

guys don't know why we ain't seen no boids, do yas? It's cuz we're too blasted fah from land. Da boids have more sense den us yoomans. We ah too fah from home, slowly goin' nuts. Look at all da ships around us. Dey stretch clean past da horizon. We're sittin' ducks for the Japs is what we are. Hey, at 17 knots, we're practically standin' still. This measly five-inch BB gun wouldn't sink a kayak." Shockley slapped the big gun with his hand like he was mad.

"A Jap kamikaze could fly right down our stacks, have breakfast wid us, and blow us to smithereens. Would that break the Admiral's haht? Naw, he wouldn't give two hoots 'n' a hollah. When the water's this smood and no wind, somethin's wrong. Heah's my advice to you victims what's losin' your minds—"

Shockley's monologue was interrupted by Cliff Smith, hollering, "Pipe down, Shockley. You're the deck ape that's going nuts, not us."

Geyer chimed in, "Shockley you're not a first class seaman, you're a first class jerk. Shut the heck up! Who do you think you are anyway?"

Shockley flashed a wiseacre grin, pulled his hat down to his right eyebrow, and jumped down from the gun mount to cast his swab over the stern and catch the biggest fish of the day. Strangely enough only moments later, the wind picked up as if blown by a giant fan. Forks of lightning stabbed the ocean beyond the horizon, while dark clouds billowed toward the *Esperance*.

From its formerly glassy smoothness, the dark blue water turned a dismal grey as swells began to rise. A gust of wind carried a couple of sailors' hats into the drink, which elicited colorful oaths from the hatless men. Our previous experience with a typhoon taught us sailors respect for the combination of wind and water, which raised an ominous sense of foreboding in those of us standing on the weather deck.

A penetrating chirp from the boatswain's pipe was immediately followed by the command, "All hands heave around and trice up! Prepare immediately for severe weather! Secure all loose gear on weather decks and below decks. Air crew, double-check all aircraft lashings on hangar deck and flight deck."

All interest in fantail swordfish immediately vanished.

"Aw, man, I've had enough of these blasted blows!" Smitty complained. "I hope to heck it ain't a bad one."

"The aerographers must've stumbled onto some scary news," Van Woodrow Wiggs offered.

Occasionally, a sailor will admit that he is totally afraid of water, even when the sea is glass smooth. Usually, they just bluster and blow a lot of hot air about toughing things out.

The commands to secure the ship were repeated as sailors dashed from one area to another in compliance with the commander's orders. Each airplane, already secured to steel pads on the flight deck by three half-inch steel cables from each landing gear, were reinforced by manila line at each landing gear.

Jack slammed his paint chipper on the deck and roared, "Those cock-eyed gold braids [commissioned officers] have to think up stupid extra stuff for us to do! With their wings folded up and nine cables securing them, nothing could tear these dad-gummed planes from the flight deck."

Everything that could be moved was lashed to the *Esperance's* deck or bulkheads. No one seemed inclined to joke as the ocean's mild swells grew into frothy peaks.

"All ship's company, below decks! No hands on weather decks!" The orders were barked out repeatedly over the ship's internal address system as well as the exterior bullhorn. Excited sailors, some pale and sweaty with fear, glided down the steel ladders to safety with newly acquired dexterity.

Salty Joe attempted to sound cool and undisturbed, declaring in a fearless tone, "Rough weather? Aw, so what?!" he jibed. "Nothing could sink this tub! Look how she handles the blow every time we leave Eulithi to head to the Philippines." But his nervous appearance at the prospect of more rough weather belied his tone.

He quickly changed his tune as we plowed smack dab into the wildest, most destructive typhoon in documented history. All officers and enlisted men in charge of ship's operations from the top, down, were taken by surprise, unable to figure out how we had cruised right into the path of a major typhoon. Ship's weathermen had seen no indication of a storm on their instruments, nor did they receive warning from any larger ships in the task unit until mere moments before the ocean turned violent.

Wind increased to a force that older, experienced seaman had never experienced. It drove spray and spume with the force of a sandblaster, removed paint from areas on the ships' hulls and superstructures. When lookouts and signalmen turned away from the blast, their cheeks and foreheads were pocked with bloody spots. This capillary bleeding was etched on the faces of every man exposed directly to the wind.

Cape Esperance was the unit flagship for our Task Unit (TU) 30.8.3. We cruised close to the north side of the storm's eye. Captain Backius, in his logistic report of December 24, 1944 reported that the *Esperance* came within approximately 10 miles of the typhoon's eye. While the very center of the eye is calm, with occasionally choppy seas and patches of blue sky, the outer edges of the eye's border—where the *Esperance* lay—the wind spews its most powerful gusts and lifts the water up into mountainous waves.

Explanation of a typhoon defies language. The closest approximation I can think of to a typhoon's wind force would be stick ones arm out an airplane window while flying 150-200 m.p.h. Author Joseph Conrad in his book *Typhoon* (written two centuries ago), and more recently Sebastian Junger, author of *The Perfect Storm,* have probably come as close as any human being in depicting the powerful combination of wind and water that constitute a typhoon.

As though suddenly seized in the gigantic paws of an underwater monster, the *Esperance* experienced upward thrusts so quick and powerful that, with nothing to grab hold of, men were slammed to the deck and slid helplessly downhill to crash into the steel bulkheads. Sailors below decks grabbed anything secure within our reach. When a severe list took too long to right itself, some men were forced to release their grip, screaming as they smashed into whatever lay in their path. There is no such thing as a soft bump on a steel ship.

Pitifully few measures are available to defend oneself from a typhoon's destruction. Hang onto something, cower, weep, cover your face, and cry out to God is just about the extent of it. I didn't really know God, having only recited aloud short bedtime prayers as a little boy with my mom.

I dreaded my turn to stand watch on the *Esperance's* open bridge. I was scared to go above decks, as the typhoon's intensity increased. Below decks, all hatches were tightly secured. Since there were no windows, I hadn't seen the waves kicking our ship around like a beach ball, nor had I felt the fiery sting of spume, a mixture of salt water, rain, and foam kicked up by the severe winds.

I shrugged into my rain gear before stepping onto the flight deck, grabbing a ladder rung made of one-inch steel rods as I attempted to climb up to the open bridge. When my hand reached the fifth or sixth rung, a gust of wind jerked me off my feet and stretched me out like a ribbon, horizontal to the flight deck. I couldn't get my legs back beneath me, no matter how frantically I tried.

Clutching the steel rung as if my life depended on it (which it did!), I felt as if the wind and spume tore at me like the Devil himself intended to throw me into the heaving sea. Youthful strength in combination with desperation and fear, evidently released enough adrenaline for me to maintain my grip. I pulled my knees up to my chin, then slowly let myself down by hand, one rung at a time, back onto the deck. As the gusts of wind diminished for second-long intervals, I flattened myself out on the deck and crawled to the interior ladder from where I could reach the open bridge without being swept overboard.

The officer of the day (OD) stood, sheltered on four sides from the typhoon's wicked fury. His face looked as though it had been chiseled in granite: above clamped lips, his nostrils flared and his eyes stared, unblinking. This lieutenant in complete charge of operations was as helpless as a toddler in a kiddy-car; his gold stripes and pins, useless. The man seemed to be completely hypnotized, unable to fathom the reality of mountains of water, canyon-like troughs, and the ferocious howling of the wind. The 10,902-ton, 512-foot-long *Cape Esperance*, fully loaded with airplanes and bombs, bounced around like a toy boat in a child's bathtub.

The *Esperance* emitted frightening snaps and groans as it bent and twisted. Would the welded seams burst, letting the ocean flood in? How much longer could the *Esperance* hold up under the punishment she was taking? Screeching from prolonged gusts too great even to be measurable by an anemometer (instrument that measures wind speed) did away with what little courage the ship's crew might have used to battle the hostile forces of nature unleashed against us.

The OD stood inside the enclosed bridge with a pair of binoculars in one hand and an unrelenting grip on something solid with the other. I couldn't imagine what he was looking for; visibility was zero, on rare occasions extending to 100 yards for a brief moment, before relapsing to zero.

"What's the wind, boatswain?" OD asked over the phone. I wondered what difference it made to know the answer.

"One hundred thirty-two knots, sir."

Shortly thereafter, a cup broke off the tip of the *Esperance's* anemometer. There would be no more reports on wind speed.

"And that last roll," the OD persisted, "how many degrees was it?"

"Forty-two degrees, sir."

Baby flattops are recognized to capsize after 38-degree rolls, top-heavy as they are even without the added weight of airplanes. Destroyers with proper ballast can return after a list of 70 degrees. Besides being nicknamed "tin cans," destroyers and destroyer escorts were also known as "over one and under two," meaning that they could cut through (under) two waves and go over the top of the next one.

Memories of my frantic experience trying to release lookout #3 from his precarious position on the catwalk still remain vivid, more than six decades later.

"Bridge, from Lookout 3. Over." I could barely hear his voice.

"Lookout 3, go ahead," I replied.

Lookout 3 requests permission to secure station. Planes coming loose above my position. Over."

"Gotcha #3. Stand by."

I leaned into the OD's protected area out of the wind in order to relay the request. "Sir, Lookout 3 reports planes loosening dangerously close to him. Looks like they're about to drop down onto the catwalk where he's located. Requests permission to secure his station."

Without so much as a glance in the direction of lookout 3, he shouted, "Not granted! We're in the middle of a battle zone! How could anybody be so dumb to not realize that?" was the OD's nonsensical response.

In weather like this, no plane—friend or foe—was flying anywhere. No one could do battle in zero visibility, while all hands struggled to save their own lives. I was sure the OD had gone insane with fear. And he called Lookout 3's request dumb? It made way more sense than the OD's response!

"Lookout 3 from bridge, negative on request to secure station. 'Zat you, Jim?"

"Bridge from 3. Ya bet yer britches this is yer buddy. You can tell that jerk with the binocs that's supposed to be in command to stick his head out and take a look at these planes. There's only one left to break loose before all five of them sweep me into the drink."

Turning to explain Jim's situation to the OD, I quickly realized it was a waste of time. Instead, I ducked out of the OD's sight and lied to Lookout 3 on the phone. "Permission granted to secure your station." I figured a few days in the brig for giving an unauthorized command was worthwhile in order to save Jim's skin, and I couldn't be busted any lower than the rank I already had.

There was no answer from Lookout 3. I repeated, "Jim, secure your station. Get the heck out of there, for the love of Pete!"

Still no answer. I leaned over the guard rail to face a gust that felt as if it intended to rip my face from my skull. I waved furiously, hoping to catch Jim's attention.

In that moment, the Esperance careened down the side of a mountainous wave into a black trough that looked as deep as Hell's Canyon in north Idaho. As the bow attempted to knife the oncoming wave, we took a deathly blow to the port side, tipping us to a starboard list which jerked three of the five Hellcats loose to crash onto the catwalk at Lookout 3 position. The heavy planes ripped the steel catwalk as though it were made of flimsy paper. A hideous roar of scraping steel rose above the howling fury of waves and wind before the planes disappeared beneath the water. Minutes later, another plane twisted around on its steel pads and plunged into the elevator well.

I stared looking for Jim on station 3, but his phones, still plugged in topside, dangled over the side, dipping in and out of the water as the ship listed. I glared at the pitiful OD, speechless with fury. I didn't dare speak. I wanted to fling myself on him and beat the life out of him.

I cried out, "God, I know you're out there someplace! No man or machinery can raise mountains of water like this or cause devastating winds to blow, and I'm not ready to meet you, wherever you are."

While being pelted with spray and spume, I wondered if God might give me some credit based on my parents' lives. Mom, a Sunday school teacher, was involved in numerous church activities. Dad, who enjoyed a reputation in Bonners Ferry as an honest business man, was a good guy to boot. He had recently gotten involved in some kind of religion that influenced him to read his Bible every morning by the kitchen stove before walking a mile to work. He even left the big book open, perhaps hoping I'd take a glance at it before going to school, but I seldom did. These things flashed through my mind in a matter of seconds.

I recalled a question being posed among the new naval recruits, "Do you think we might be killed one of these days while we're in this cock-eyed Navy?"

"Holy smoke, man! You don't have to join the military to get sent to hell. You can get killed crossing the street," one of the recruits answered.

Another added, "I doggone near got killed when I took a spill on my skis last winter."

A third recruit chuckled before adding his two cents' worth, "My old man came close to finishing me off when he beat the tar out of me the time I came in at 2:00 a.m. from a date."

I felt obligated to contribute to this intellectual exchange, so I said, "I figured I'd die some day from eating Ma's leftovers, but I wish I had some now!"

7

You've heard some tales of violent gales, and storms on all seacoasts
And some believe that all big storms are wicked pirate ghosts.
But this one is no legend from an ancient sailor's boast;
But a living account of a big typhoon, far from the China coast.

The worst one ever seen by man in a hundred years or more;
It happened in December of nineteen forty-four.
'Twas on one Tuesday morning, the sea was getting rough;
And while the sailors seemed not to mind, for they were seasoned and tough.

And many had seen the hardships that all sailor men must see;
But none had faced a hardship like the crazy China Sea.
Then, later in the afternoon, the sea was getting worse;
And some of the sailors began to growl and some of them to curse.

But very soon thereafter, the boys had changed their minds.
And some of them were asking, would their Savior please be kind?
For nothing else in all the world is even half so cruel
As heading into a big typhoon, then running out of fuel.

And then be jerked and twisted until the seams begin to break,
While trapped like rats by the crazy sea, with all our lives at stake
In waves so high they must have reached a hundred feet or more
We knew that we were knocking on old Davy Jones's door.

There wasn't a man on board who didn't think this wasn't our last trip;
Then a miracle happened along and saved the good old ship.
And now we stand in sad repast for the poor lads who went down
Who well deserved the title to their promised harps and crowns.

So let us hope that old St. Pete was there to see them off
And make sure they were all secure before he went aloft.
And while the storm was at its worst, the angry sea we fought;
A lot of things were on my mind, but this was my prime thought:

Oh, Lady Luck, please lend your oar to a frightened sailor's plea
And deliver me from the evil hands of the crazy China sea!
For twice it is we just escaped the wicked old witch's grasp
And if I have been sinful, please listen to my last gasp.
Just take me back to my lady love, where no more storm I'll fear,
And then I'll sail in Central Park, where land is always near.
Author H.N. Miller, BM 2/C, USS Cape Esperance (from onboard ship news flyer)

Outside, with little protection from the onslaught, no one was more helpless than I. Sixty-two feet above water level on an open bridge, driving rain mixed with salt water scraped at my face. With one hand, I held my earphones in place to maintain communication with lookouts stationed on the catwalk, barely able to see past their own noses; my other hand clutched a one-inch-thick vertical pipe to hold myself against the ship's bulkhead and keep myself from being blown over the bridge's seemingly laughable "safety" rail and into the churning water.

The storm battering from the ship's port side rolled

the *Esperance* so far to starboard, we scooped up tons of water in the 40mm gun tubs on the catwalk. Seeing those tubs filled with water frightened the dickens out of me, for I was second loader on one of them.

Our ship was fearfully top-heavy, even without a load, but the huge flight deck now held 32 combat-ready airplanes. The flight deck acted like a big shovel as the *Esperance* plowed into the sides of salt water mountains scooping up three to four feet of water, which turned into a river that rushed the length of the flight deck, tugging at the scores of planes moored there.

Our ship was hurled into the broad side of mountainous waves like a spear from the hand of a mighty warrior. With little or no water parting at the bow, the *Esperance* stopped in a virtual head-on collision, followed by a violent shudder, then a roll to starboard that seemed interminable. Megatons of water bombarded the ship's squared-off stern causing unexpected forward thrusts, opposite to head-on resistance. A lengthy pause while heeled 45 degrees to starboard felt like an eternity, I knew there was no way the *Esperance* could possibly right itself. Had one more big wave slapped the ship's side during this vulnerable moment with her gun tubs full of water, the *Esperance* could easily have capsized.

Our bow was boosted to breathtaking heights, nearly standing the *Esperance* on end. Waves had reached such steepness, we held our breath for fear of toppling over backward (called pitch-poling). Sudden changes of altitude from the tops of the waves to the depths of the troughs caused ears to alternately plug and pop.

Teetering on wave peaks, the *Esperance's* two giant propellers were lifted completely out of the water. Engine revolutions increased while the props churned in the air, free of resistance until they could bite into water again resulting in scary vibrations throughout the ship. On the open bridge, I didn't realize at first what was causing the extreme shaking. I thought the hull had split open, and peered over the edge of my railing for any sign of the *Esperance* settling deeper into the water on its way down to "Davy Jones Locker" on the ocean's floor.

Airplanes parked on carriers' flight decks windmilled at 100 to 200 rpm's in the path of unstoppable forces of nature. Airplane wings were torn from fuselages and swept into the sea. The planes themselves pulled at their cable fastenings, eventually ripping loose. Steel cables and manila lines were rendered useless as the flight deck's steel pads snapped, releasing the planes a few at a time to crash into each other before being tossed into the sea.

Captain Bockius reported to the Third Fleet's flagship that the *Esperance* lost steering control and couldn't maneuver with the Task Unit. At this point, Admiral Halsey ordered the cruiser USS Miami and destroyer USS Thorne to stand by in case the Esperance capsized.

A captain on one of the destroyers in our task unit mentioned that in a wild storm, the tendency is to exaggerate the height of giant waves. He noted that his ship's flying bridge is 45 feet above waterline, with the top of the mast a full 93 feet from the water line. The same class of destroyer next to the *Esperance* in formation was occasionally visible from our ship. From the captain's position on the bridge, when both ships were in the trough, the tip of the adjacent ship's mast disappeared entirely behind a wave's crest, which meant that the waves battering the *Esperance* were in excess of 93 feet!

A civil engineer friend, full of geometric knowledge, calculated that the distance of sway on the *Esperance's* open bridge from even keel; (perpendicular) to a 42-degree heel would be an arc of 63 feet, the same as the distance from where I stood on the ship's bridge to water level. Many times, however, the *Esperance* took lists past perpendicular to port side which increased the distance of the arc to 85-90 feet. Those 90 feet gave me—and surely, the officer of the day a sense of overwhelming helplessness. As I gripped more firmly to the metal pipe, I closed my eyes at frequent intervals in order to avoid seeing the wild water. My internal voice cried at each list, "She's not going to stop! She's not going to stop until she rolls over!"

The extended sway below deck near the pivotal area, where most of the ship's crew clung for dear life, wasn't felt as strongly as on the bridge. But it would be nearly impossible for the boys below decks to escape to a life raft, should the Esperance actually capsize. Wild as it was on the weather deck, it provided the only chance to abandon ship if the *Esperance* should go down.

Multiplied tons of water driven by merciless gusts of wind ripped wings, cowlings, and cabins from the brand-new fighter planes as though they were no more than balsa wood. With as little effort as it takes to sweep the front porch with a broom, tons of heavy wreckage screeched across the flight deck and over the side. To see and hear this was to watch any hope of survival disappear beneath the waves with the airplanes. But the loss of tons of weight from high up on the flight deck lowered the Esperance's center of gravity, which increased the ship's stability.

On the flight deck of the *USS Cape Esperance*, a plane suddenly jerked loose from its mooring and was thrown atop one of the stacks at the foot of the tower (island), where it burst into flames. An American news reporter trying to get a glimpse of the weather above decks, saw this happen and scurried below in a hurry. The fire was extinguished within minutes by heavy rain and spume.

Noon chow had been served just before the main force of the typhoon hit, spelling chaos in capital letters. Hot coffee sloshing out of giant urns scalded some of the cooks. Heavy tables, steel trays, benches, and broken dishes piled up on the starboard side of the dining hall. The floor, smeared with greasy pork, gravy and butter, rendered it impossible for sailors to keep their footing. Anyone in chow hall who didn't have hold of something solid when the storm hit, was flung down into the slimy mess, or slammed against the *Esperance's* steel bulkheads to suffer bruises, cuts, and broken bones.

Treating the injured was all but impossible during Typhoon Cobra; the ship's sick bay couldn't keep up with the unrelenting flow of injured men. Passageway decks were lined with outstretched sailors, awaiting their turn to be treated. Water backed up in the toilets being used by those suffering seasickness. Ventilation was shut off because of the danger posed by gasoline fumes spreading and igniting. All but the ship's dim red emergency lights were extinguished. As a result, men collided in the near-darkness, triggering outbursts of swearing and fist-fights from tempers already frayed by the tempest.

Bibles that had never seen the light of day since their owners boarded ship—like mine, for example—suddenly appeared in the trembling hands of sailors convinced they were on the verge of death. Rugged men and immature teens alike wept openly, fear overcoming their natural hesitance to express emotion. Prayers spilled from the lips of men who normally spouted foul oaths, desperately pleading with a God they neither knew nor wanted anything to do with—until there was no other hope.

I took the Bible my mother gave me at the *Cape Esper-*

ance's commissioning in Astoria, from my locker and flipped through the pages. I didn't know what to look for among the tongue-twisting names. I started with the Gospel of Matthew, the first book in the New Testament, which didn't do much to whet my appetite to continue reading. But just holding a Bible would, I hoped, help me sort of square things with God.

I recalled letters from my sister-in-law, Fran, with notes added by my brother, John: "Paul, we are praying that some day you will enjoy the Christian life we are privileged to enjoy." Another letter informed me that Christ died for my sins. I had thought, *So, what?* But now I was anxious to get below decks and reread those letters, if only the *Esperance* remained afloat long enough!

John's question to me, posed when I was only sixteen and visiting with him and Fran during my few days of vacation, kept booming through my mind as though being announced on the *Esperance's* bull horn. "Paul, are you saved? Paul, are you saved?" I had sassed John at the time; his simple question now haunted me. I didn't know what to do. Although I didn't even really know what he meant, I knew I wasn't the kind of "saved" John talked about. If I could be saved from this killer typhoon, maybe I could find out about the other "saved" that John and Fran constantly talked about.

Years later, my friend and former shipmate, George Frantz, gunner on the five-inch cannon who also served watch on the open bridge of the *Esperance*, shared his experience with me.

"I was getting bumped and slammed against the bulkhead on my way down the passage to my station on the open bridge. It was while the ship was taking her most extreme rolls to the starboard side. The wind was fierce, and I was scared. I knew there was a strong possibility that I wouldn't live much longer.

"I stopped, knelt down in the passageway, and offered a prayer to God, asking Him to look out for my mother. I immediately felt the warmth and comfort that my mother had always given me. Later in the day, the wind subsided, and I knew my prayer was answered."

*   *   *

I was startled when an officer popped out of the ladder hole, his fancy hat pulled on so tight it distorted his features. I didn't recognize him as he crawled on all fours in front of me, hand grabbing at the guard rail. It was our skipper, Captain Robert Bockius. Still on his knees, head just above the rail, he peered over the edge and was rewarded for his trouble by a strong blast of stinging rain. As the *Esperance* took a bad list to starboard, the Skipper glanced back at the catwalk and saw the 40mm gun tubs fill with water. He yelped, "Oh, God!" twice before crawling back down the ladder hole.

He immediately ordered 300 petrified sailors to the port side of the hangar deck, contributing some 45,000 pounds of ballast to help offset the extreme rolls. Three news correspondents were happy to leave the bridge and contribute their weight to the effort. The Skipper then sent his orderly below to release all prisoners from the brig, typically the last act preceding an order to abandon ship.

Watch on the open bridge was four hours on and four hours off, while our little "jeep carrier" was tossed around like a toy. After Captian Bockius reported our steerage loss, the *Esperance* was sucked into the typhoon's eyebrow, too close to the eye, where we were thrown around like a wood chip, jerked, twisted, and tipped unmercifully. We could do nothing but hang on in the very center, unaware that the destroyer USS Hull already had lost its struggle and had sunk.

I couldn't even speak when standing in the wind. My lips felt as if they were being ripped off, while the wind all but gagged me, making sound impossible. I pulled myself against the bulkhead of the OD's cabin, which removed some of the sting from the evil portside blasts. I was infuriated that the OD wouldn't permit me to enter his cabin, mere inches away and boasting plenty of room, not to mention providing a modicum of protection from the fierce onslaught of Nature.

I found myself conscience-stricken over my anger at the OD. He could've been doing what many of the rest of us were: trying to concentrate on something besides drowning or being ripped apart by sharks. Never before had I been in a situation where I was certain, deep down, that I would die. While bitten by the sharp teeth of wind and rain, dozens of past experiences that replayed in my mind only increased my feelings of guilt.

I tried to blame my loving mother's methods of discipline during my childhood; she used a combination of fear and guilt, to great effect. Before I ate a meal one day, she said, "Spit your gum out into this napkin." But I had already swallowed it.

"Ma, it's already gone."

"What??? Never. Swallow. Your. Gum. If you keep doing that, the doctor will have to cut a hole in your stomach with a knife to get the ball of gum out." Months passed before I forgot and swallowed my gum again, and I tried everything I could think of to vomit it back up.

Another time Mom said, "My stars and garters, little man! How much cinnamon are you putting on your toast? If you put too much on, it will dry up your blood." Wow! I had seen smears of blood, nearly the same color as dried cinnamon, and was fully grown before I could

69

enjoy a piece of cinnamon toast without fear.

"Heavens to Betsy!" was one of Mom's favorite expressions, and one I heard frequently. It was my job to entertain the little kids brought by their mothers to the Methodist Ladies' Aid society.

"Heavens to Betsy, Pauly! Will you stop swinging that poor little kid in a circle?"

"Golly, Ma! We just wanted to get dizzy is all."

"Swinging him in a circle like that will give that poor boy an enlarged liver," Mom retorted.

I tried to avoid the little kid, for fear he would look like a skeleton next time I saw him. But when I caught a glimpse of him on several occasions, I checked him out unobtrusively. Was he pale? Talking funny? Cross-eyed? I was relieved not to spot any abnormal symptoms.

Being alone on the bridge of the *Esperance* was taking its toll on me. The OD remained inside his protected area, clearly not including seaman Paul in his list of worthy shipmates. If all hands had been ordered below decks, I was never notified. And if the OD had been given such an order, why didn't he send me below? With no one to talk to, there was no interrupting the deep conviction and despondency over my actions during 18 years of existence.

I had lied to my parents. I left home against their will at the age of 16. I had stolen cash from my hard-working Dad, which made me feel worse than seasick. I shoplifted during my stint with the high school band and the drum and bugle corps on trips to other towns. I was even proud of the filthy vocabulary I had accumulated.

More recently, during the few months I'd been aboard the *Esperance*, I had been transferred to the Exec's office as yeoman striker because my record showed I could type. This was an opportunity for me to be promoted to wearing one red stripe on my sleeve and a small raise in

pay. However, during my time at that job, I was dishonest.
I was to prepare lists and records for accused sailors required to appear before the Commander at Exec's mast
for trial. I was also given responsibility of Liberty Card
Yeoman, keeping track of which divisions were free to
leave the ship and issue ID cards to those men.

One evening, a cook approached me with a big, toothy
smile asking why I couldn't let all but one or two cooks
have liberty cards.

"Schlener," he said, laying a heavy hand on my shoulder, his face close enough that the scent of onions wafted
into my nostrils, "one cook will be enough in case some
'gold braid' gets hungry before bedtime. But that never
happens, mate."

"Good grief, man! If I get caught, I'll be the one doing
time in the brig, not you." I argued, backing off to draw a
breath of fresh air and allow my left shoulder to recover
from the ponderous weight of his hand.

"We'll make it worth your while, mate," he promised.
"We have a stack of Virginia ham a mile high, and eggs by
the ton. There's always a pile of bread and butter left over,
and you guys already have a hot plate in the office. I'll get
you a frying pan. You'll never run out of goodies!"

And so I agreed to accommodate the heavy-handed
cook and his pals. I started dishing out liberty cards, making sure at least one cook stayed on board "just in case."
Everything hummed along fine... until somebody
squealed. Scared stiff, I wondered if I was destined to become the *Cape Esperance's* first burial at sea. I wasn't ordered to Captain's or Exec's mast for trial. Instead, from
higher up the chain, a four-word order filtered down to
the officer in charge of Exec's office: "Get rid of
Schlener."

8

"The seas have lifted up, O Lord, the seas have lifted up their voice; the seas have lifted up their pounding waves. Mightier than the thunder of the great waters, mightier than the breakers of the sea, the Lord on high is mighty" Psalm 93:3-4 NIV.

The chief petty officer showed me the paper that transferred me to Damage Control Office. I knew why without asking, and was glad for the transfer. Better to transfer than do extra duty in the bilges or spend time in the brig! There was little enough to do in Damage Control, apart from hope we weren't torpedoed or attacked by a *kamikaze.* My main duty consisted of handing out material like rubber boots, parkas, and raincoats to those who produced request slips signed by their superior officers.

I don't know why I didn't get caught, because I simply

transferred from one area of dishonesty to another. The cooks were decked out in the best hooded windbreakers, raincoats, and parkas to be found on the *Esperance*.

"Hey, Slenna," hollered one of the cooks who had enjoyed several illegal liberties, thanks to me. "We radda have da liberty cahds den rain coats." I even helped myself to a parka that I took home with me when I was discharged. I felt so guilty later on, I wrote a letter to the U.S. Navy confessing my theft and asking how to pay or otherwise make amends. I'm sure it made whoever read it laugh, although I never received a response. At least I had appeased my conscience.

But in the midst of Cobra, a reminiscent review of my wayward life didn't have any effect on the storm outside. The *Esperance's* twin propellers, one full-power ahead, the other in reverse, couldn't turn the ship into the wind. I was sure that within a matter of minutes, I would be in eternity, whatever that meant. *What was drowning like,* I wondered. *Was it painful? How long would it take?* Being pulled under water and torn apart by sharks wasn't a pleasant prospect.

I had attended church often enough to have heard about heaven and hell. I knew I didn't qualify for heaven, for sure! No use in my trying to weasel-word in a feeble effort to persuade God to let me get my foot in the door. From practice, I knew hell as a cuss word, and figured it was the opposite of heaven.

In the midst of the typhoon, I recalled Reverend Pike, recently appointed to the Methodist pastorate in Bonners Ferry before I left home. He had stopped me on the street just after I enlisted in the Navy, towering over me wearing glasses so thick they looked like tiny fishbowls. However, his six-foot-plus height advantage kept me from making any smart remarks, and I attempted to hurry past with a simple, "Hi, Rev. Pike."

But he stopped, offering a large paw to shake. I attempted to side-step to avoid further conversation, but again he stood in my path.

"Your mother mentioned that you joined the Navy," he said.

"Yes sir, I did. I passed the physical—nothing more than presenting a live body and making my way clear across the examining room to the physician. I'm fit as a fiddle, and just waiting for my call to active duty."

Rev. Pike flashed a quick smile, then quickly turned serious again. "Well, Paul, I wish you well as you enter the service. I respect you for the desire to defend our country."

His pleasant attitude disarmed me, which made the follow-up feel like a sucker punch. "What I wish you would do, Paul, is make a decision for Christ before you go into active duty. Ships go down, you know, and some of the boys don't make it back home."

"I'll just have to take my chances!" I remarked, making good my escape. I wondered, on the open bridge of the *Cape Esperance* as Typhoon Cobra blasted all around me, if I would be one of the boys who would make it back home.

Over and over, I thought of Mom and Dad: Dad pounding out hymns and ragtime with his calloused fingers on the old upright piano until Mom called him for supper. I sometimes accompanied him on my snare drum. Would I ever set foot in Dad's leather shop again, catch a whiff of handmade leather goods or run my hands over a just-completed saddle? What I wouldn't give to have just one minute in Mom's full fridge... I'd go upstairs and check out my attic loft, practice on my cheap wooden drums until Ma thumped from the ceiling below with a broom handle.

When will I have another opportunity to slip into the Fountain Café for a cup of coffee and a piece of pie, maybe for another glimpse of that cute waitress, Jessie MacDonald? I couldn't forget her, no matter how hard I tried. And admittedly, I didn't give it serious effort. Just saying her name was music to my ears, for a few moments displacing the roar of wind and water. She was just the right size at five feet, two inches. Although I never knew what to say to girls in high school, and the old photos prove I was never what could be construed as the answer to a maiden's prayers. In a gym full of cute gals, Jessie stood out at high school mixers like a bouquet of fresh flowers on an empty table. I'm sure lots of other fellas thought she was a nice gal, runner-up for homecoming queen that year. I dreaded never making it back to Bonners Ferry to enjoy a date with that special young lady.

My reveries of home ended abruptly at 4:00 a.m. when my arm was grabbed from behind. I nearly flew off the bridge.

"Jason, you are the biggest jerk that ever came out of New Jersey!" I yelled at my lookout relief. "Boy, you scared me, but am I ever glad to see you."

Jason kept a tight grip on his rain jacket so he wouldn't lose it to the typhoon. With eyes squinted to mere slits, he peered over the edge to get a better look at the turbulence.

"Oh, man! Is she getting rough, or is she getting rough?" he hollered, dropping to his haunches and wagging his head in disbelief. Jason was getting a look at this violent storm for the first time. It was frightful enough below decks, with severe teeter-tottering that spilled men from their bunks. But there was no comparison to seeing—and feeling—it from up high.

"I'm on edge like never before," I told Jason. "Small as I am, I must be the biggest chicken on this hunk of steel.

Watching those five planes tear off the catwalk and drop into the drink with Jim made me sick. Take a gander at the catwalk where lookout 3 used to be."

Jason's reaction was everything I could've hoped for. "Holy Mackerel! There's no sight or sound of any of this below decks. God help us all!"

I warned him, "Just wait until we take a nosedive into the next canyon. She scoops up at least three feet of water over the flight deck. Both props come clean out of the water, then shake us like an earthquake when they bite the water again."

Jason expressed his relief. "Below decks it feels like this tub is cracking in two. As long as the trembling is *just* the propellers, I feel a lot better."

We had to yell so loud to make ourselves heard over the din, the blood vessels stood out on our necks.

Jason noticed that the ship seemed to bend in the middle and twist. I agreed, revealing my anxiety.

"I don't know what keeps this tub from busting in half! I tell ya, man, I'm not ready to meet God almighty, and it looks like we might have to any minute. I sure as heck don't want to get dumped into that wild water."

Jason shifted his weight to his knees, as he said, "Schlener, you talk about not being ready to meet God. What about me, man? I've been nothing but trouble all my life."

I was glad to hand over the phones to Jason and go below. Staggering down the passageway toward the stern, I grabbed overhead beams and pipes to avoid slamming into the bulkheads whenever the *Esperance* returned from a list. Ponderous mountains of water from the port side shoved us 30 and 40 degrees to starboard, striking the ship's crew with agonizing fear that the ship would never return to upright. Some vomited from seasickness, and others from the utter hopelessness that they wouldn't survive the savage storm. Everyone begged God to bring the ship back to level.

*   *   *

The destroyer *USS Hull*, DD350, one of the *Esperance's* partners in Task Unit 30.8.3 cruised close to us. Skipper Jim Marks, a short man with dark hair and eyes and an olive complexion, assumed command of the *Hull* a scant three months before going to war with Typhoon Cobra. The *Hull* had done more than its share of knocking Japanese fighter planes and kamikazes out of the sky, and sinking a small schooner near Guadalcanal. She had seen action during the Aleutian campaign, the Marshall and Gilbert Islands operations, and took part in the "Great Marianas turkey shoot" of June 19, 1944.

TU 30.8.3 was drawn close to the edge of the typhoon's eye where the most powerful gusts became veritable killers. Captain Calhoun, skipper of destroyer *USS Dewey*, and various aerographers estimated Typhoon Cobra's gusts exceeded 200 knots, a fact borne out by books on oceanography and seamanship which confirm that gusts near a typhoon's eye reach an excess of 200 knots. A mere 110 knots of wind generates seventy-eight pounds of pressure per square foot of sail area; the *USS Hull*, with approximately 600 square feet of sail on just the one stack, reached 23 tons of steady pressure. It's no wonder her motor whaleboat was smashed, torn away, and dumped into the water. Depth charges were snatched from the K-gun mountings. Her skipper hoped the wind would blow the stacks off the Hull to lower the ship's center of gravity and diminish the wind's thrust.

With visibility at zero to less than 100 yards, those of us on the Esperance couldn't even see the Hull, maneuvering near us. At around 11:30 a.m. on December 18, the tough little destroyer lost steering control, but was still able to recover from lurch and heel of 60 degrees.

A quick pitch to starboard tore the junior officer of the day from his post, and flung him—airborne—to the starboard side of the *Hull's* pilot house. Just after noon, the ship rolled to an incredible 70 degrees, pugnaciously righting itself to continue battling the typhoon.

Closer to the eye of the storm at the north end of the typhoon, violence was at its worst with merciless gusts of wind at velocities impossible to measure. Men were battered against steel bulkheads and decks as the *Hull* was kicked from stem to stern. Sailors clung desperately to whatever they could catch hold of, hardly daring to think that their ship might sink. Some cursed non-stop, while others prayed fervently. Young men sobbed uncontrollably, convinced they would never see their loved ones again.

Again the destroyer took a list of 70 degrees, but the gale suddenly subsided and she sat up straight. Only minutes later, the devilish wind exploded in a sustained, overpowering gust that heeled her past 70 degrees until she lay on her starboard side. Sea water rushed into the pilot house and through every open ventilation duct. Like a prize fighter knocked out cold by his opponent, the *Hull* was finished.

Skipper Jim Marks stayed on the port side of the bridge where he observed his panic-stricken crew clambering to parts of the destroyer that remained above water. A short time later, he stepped off into the water, feeling the concussion of the *Hull's* exploding boilers and the tremendous suction as the ship sank. Of the 263 personnel on board, approximately 100 were trapped below decks, unable to escape. Sixty-two men were ultimately rescued from the ocean.

Skipper Marks impressed at least one fellow naval officer as a serious man who operated strictly according to regulation; excellent qualities when trouble lurks around the corner, but not always conducive to heightening crew morale. He was admired by the captain of a sister ship for the quality of his performance at sea and the appearance of his vessel. Phone calls from survivors of the *USS Hull* and articles written by surviving officers after the ship's tragic loss, agreed that Captain Marks was an extremely bad skipper and the sole reason his ship sank. Jim Marks, the *Hull's* most unpopular commanding officer, took his own life at the age of 71 by a self-inflicted gunshot wound to the head.

*　　*　　*

A veteran of the Japanese attack on Pearl Harbor, the destroyer *USS Monaghan*, DD 354 rammed, depth-charged, and sank a Japanese submarine. She also participated in the battles of the Coral Sea, Midway, Marshall Islands, the Gilberts, and the Philippine Sea. Bruce Garrett, new commander of the Monaghan, was remembered by a naval academy classmate as the smallest and youngest-looking in his class. On active duty, he was a quiet officer with a friendly smile, dignified and well liked by his entire crew. He handled his ship like a veteran, although he had assumed command of the Monaghan only ten days before facing Typhoon Cobra.

Having served on other ships, Garrett had seen rough weather before, but nothing compared to the poison of Cobra. The *Monaghan's* serious problems were noticed at 9:27 a.m. on December 17th by sister destroyers in the task unit when the *Monaghan* reported inability to steer the assigned course. Captain Jasper Acuff, commander of task group 30.8, advised Garrett to use more speed to facilitate steering. In hindsight, more speed turns out to have been bad advice.

At 9:36 a.m. Garrett called Acuff in reply, "Unable to

come to base course. I've tried full speed, but it will not work." The next message from the *Monaghan* was that she was totally out of control, her generators failed which rendered the steering motor inoperative. From 11:15 a.m. on, *Monaghan* was dead in the water, helpless against the overpowering assault of Typhoon Cobra.

By 11:30 a.m. the *Monaghan* was so beaten and twisted that some of the overhead spaces in the engine room and fire room ripped loose. Fifty men fought their way to the aft gun shelter for protection, and hung on as best they could.

A few prayed aloud, "Don't let us down now, dear Lord. Bring it back, oh God. Bring it back!"

Whenever the ship survived a severe roll, the men shouted, "Thanks, dear Lord!"

The end came around 12:30 p.m. When the ship's heavy gun shelter hatch was thrown open, men straggled out as quickly as they could. Those standing on the side of the ship hung on as long as they could, until their strength flagged. Those who let go were beaten to a pulp as the waves repeatedly slammed them against the ship's hull.

One struggling survivor was fast losing strength when a shipmate hollered to him, "Hey, Ralph, grab that life raft in back of you!" Ralph made it to the raft and was later rescued. But the shipmate who guided him to the raft and took time to help others out of the gun shelter had part of his foot torn off and was stripped naked by the force of a whirlpool as the Monaghan sank. Blue from cold and loss of blood, the poor boy grew delirious before breathing his last. One of the boys on the raft said a prayer before their first burial at sea. Sixteen officers and 235 enlisted men on the *USS Monaghan* were taken to watery graves; only six were rescued.

* * *

New, sleek and swift, the famous destroyer *USS Spence*, DD512, was a beautiful ship. Her powerful (sixty thousand horsepower) engines shoved her two thousand and fifty tons of steel a mite faster than most of her sister ships, although with a quicker rate of fuel consumption. Other destroyers in the *Spence's* group were older, smaller, and powered by a mere forty-two thousand, eight hundred horsepower engines. The officers and men on board were proud of the *Spence* and all the victories she'd won in battles against Japan. She earned a Presidential Citation while fighting with the Little Beaver Squadron in the Solomon Islands.

Spence's stability was excellent in rough water when her fuel tanks were topped off, giving her well-trained crew a sense of security. The faster ship had to refuel more frequently with such huge engines. None of the crew entertained the idea that their stellar ship could roll over and sink; bombs, torpedoes, depth charges, and *kamikazes* might pose a threat, but no mere wave could ever do her in.

On December 17, when Typhoon Cobra took the Third Fleet by surprise, *USS Spence* was caught in the clutches of the toughest water she had ever experienced while at the same time, unfortunately, low on fuel. *Spence* dogged the trail of the task group oiler, hoping the unpredictable hit and run blasts of the typhoon would give the *Spence* enough calm in order to refuel. Instead, the force of the storm increased. Side-by-side refueling was out of the question, as the ship and tanker would collide. An attempt to refuel by the stern method proved impossible when the fuel line separated after fifteen minutes of struggle.

The unlucky destroyer, so light without a full fuel load, perched too high above the water line and was subject to catching more wind. Captain Acuff, commander of the refueling-at-sea organization, had personally ordered the *Spence* to refuel the morning of December 17. For whatever reason, his order was never carried out. Later on, the ship's skipper decided not to take on sea water for ballast, expecting to be able to refuel later on. (Captains of ships at sea—like kings—have the last word in any decision.)

On the morning of December 18, however, Typhoon Cobra increased with such force, no accurate wind velocity measurements could be taken. Ditto for degrees of ships' lists and heights of the mountainous waves they faced. In the heat of the moment, nobody cared about numbers or percentages; staying alive was uppermost in everyone's minds for, if a ship went down, chances of surviving on the open sea were slim to none. The struggle to keep ships afloat against impossible odds sapped energy from some of the strongest sailors. Even then, lives were lost in the effort.

At 9:00 a.m. on the 18th, all hope for the *USS Spence* to take on fuel was abandoned. One boiler was shut down to conserve the remaining fuel, slowing the ship to eight knots. At that speed, she could keep moving for twenty-four hours. At that time, the decision was made to take on sea water for ballast, but it came too late.

At 10:00 a.m., the *Spence* was caught between mammoth swells while screeching winds held her broadside to the onslaught of pounding waves. With each smashing blow, windows on the bridge shattered, allowing in tons of water and effectively eliminating what little visibility the helmsman had. Tons of accelerated sea water shot across the superstructure and threw the whaleboat, along with any moveable gear, into the ocean. The *Spence* was completely out of control, at the mercy of a decidedly unmerciful sea.

The ship's chief machinist reported that the *Spence*

suddenly took a roll of 72-75 degrees, tipped for about ten seconds, and then righted herself. At noon, during the few minutes Jason and I were shouting at one another on the bridge of the *Cape Esperance*, the *Spence* rolled all the way over on her side. She remained there for roughly seven minutes, capsized, broke in half, and disappeared into the sea, taking nearly all of her crew with her.

More than 200 sailors went down with the ship; many more drowned while attempting to locate something to cling to. Those lucky enough to find life jackets, float nets, or pneumatic belts were blown so far from the helpless ship, they couldn't even see her when the *Spence* sank. A small group of floundering men on a makeshift raft helped each other as best they could in their struggle to stay alive while violent winds flipped them over and over. All the men were exhausted; those unconscious helped by those who remained alert. In spite of all their efforts, several men died. Two five-gallon kegs of fresh water were lashed to the raft, but the medical kit and two food kits were lost.

The survivors grew exhilarated when they spotted two search planes. Sadly, the men's whistling, yelling, and waving proved futile. Without the raft's flares and dye kits to draw the planes' attention, the survivors remained invisible to their would-be rescuers.

On December 20, an aircraft carrier spotted the *Spence's* survivors on their float net. Totally despondent at having lost almost all of their shipmates, the men were relieved to think that they were about to enjoy rest, medical attention, and clean clothing from the ship's store. Hot meals from the galley, candy, cigarettes, beer and pop would be bountifully supplied aboard the big ship, they knew. But the carrier didn't even slow down, not wanting to become a sitting duck for submarines and risk the lives of several thousand men. Instead, lookouts on the ship spotted the makeshift raft, setting off smoke bombs and flares as they steamed on by.

The survivors' wilted spirits soared to an all-time high when a destroyer appeared on the horizon shortly after the flattop passed them by. But it searched in the wrong directions, resulting in still more disheartenment and the sense that rescue would never come. Some of the men swore in loud voices, while others prayed to God.

Suddenly, their prayers were answered. They whooped loud thanks to high heaven as a destroyer escort appeared, headed straight for them as though the destroyer was a fish they were reeling in to their raft. The *USS Swearer, DE 186*, proved to be a Godsend. Other brave men from the *Spence* were rescued by two other destroyer escorts, to number 24 survivors out of the total 633 valiant men who had served aboard the *USS Spence*.

Sister ships of the same class as Esperance show damage from the storm

9

Fear not that the whirlwind shall carry thee hence,
Nor wait for its onslaught in breathless suspense,
Nor shrink from the whips of the terrible hail,
But pass through the edge to the heart of the gale,
For there is a shelter, sunlighted and warm,
And Faith sees her God through the eye of the storm.

The passionate tempest with rush and wild roar
And threatenings of evil may beat on the shore,
The waves may be mountains, the fields battle plains,
And the earth be immersed in a deluge of rains,
Yet, the soul stayed on God may sing bravely its psalm,
For the heart of the storm is the center of calm.

Let hope be not quenched in the blackness of night,
Though the cyclone awhile may have blotted the light,
For behind the great darkness the stars ever shine,

And the light of God's heavens, His love shall make thine.
Let no gloom dim thine eyes, but uplift them on high
To the face of God and the blue of His sky.

The storm is thy shelter from danger and sin,
And God Himself takes thee for safety within;
The tempest with Him passeth into deep calm,
And the roar of the winds is the sound of a psalm.
Be glad and serene when the tempest clouds form;
God smiles on His child in the eye of the storm.

(~Streams in the Desert, p126. Author not mentioned)

At the end of the passageway sat a panic-stricken sailor that had been nicknamed Gramps because of his advanced age of 32, and already being a husband and father to three children. None of us deck apes could figure out why in the world he joined the Navy at such an old age! An agreeable friend to all the Second Division sailors, Gramps was so severely taxed by Typhoon Cobra, he went temporarily berserk.

Gramps fumbled with the tangled straps and cords of the five life preservers he had strung around himself, his girth ballooning to nearly twice that of the hatch. When he spotted me coming down the passageway, he seized a crowbar in his right and brandished it with unmistakable menace. I stopped short, cringing when he exploded with a screech of profanity. Gramps grabbed a port latch handle with one hand and managed to hoist himself upright, offering more space to wield the crowbar in his other hand.

"Don't try to move me away from this hatch, or I'll kill you!" he threatened. "Don't even come close, or I'll bash your brains in with this crowbar. If you don't believe me, just try! I'm tellin' ya, don't even act friendly. I'm the first son-of-a-gun out the hatch when this bucket of slop tips over. You hearing me?"

The poor guy was insane with fear, but a smashing wave that walloped us from the port side and tipped us near to capsizing, ended his discourse as he squeezed his eyes shut and held his breath until we began to return from the list.

"I hear you, Gramps," I assured him. "Slow down and relax. I'm all for you, man! We're all in the same bucket, you know." I remained at a safe distance, keeping a wary eye out in case he decided to chuck the crowbar at me. I inched past him, spouting my layman's counsel. "You gotta get back to your family, Gramps. I know that. For sure you'll make it with all those life preservers strapped to you."

I headed in the opposite direction down the passageway, offering one last comment: "Good luck, partner."

I felt sorry for Gramps. If he really needed to get through the hatchway, he would get stuck there, blocking the way of others attempting to escape if the Esperance should capsize. But nobody wanted to risk trying to move him.

I hurried to my compartment and pulled out some of the letters from sister-in-law Fran that I stored in my locker. I pored over them as the *Esperance* continued to list and lurch. I searched for a sentence or two that would tell me what to do in order to get on the good side of "the Man upstairs" as I'd heard some people refer to God, or how to make a decision for Christ.

I was back on the open bridge when the captain called for all hands to port side of the hangar deck for ballast in a frantic effort to keep the old tub from capsizing. Seven hundred sailors would offer approximately fifty tons of ballast. I wondered how much help that would be. From my position, I didn't see the effort, if it ever occurred; climbing while the ship was at a 35-40 degree list would've been nearly impossible. Although an American journalist on board noted that he went to contribute to the effort.

Lookout stations were secured, and Captain Bockius suggested to Commander McDonald that a crew with cable-cutters free the remaining airplanes that dangled loosely on the flight deck. Doing so would lower the *Cape Esperance's* center of gravity and diminish the ship's top-heaviness. Commander McDonald refused, deeming it too risky for sailors to work in the full force of the typhoon's wind, and the idea was abandoned.

Shortly after these emergency measures were adopted, the storm slowly moved away. By 6:00 a.m. on December 19, the ocean was calm. It was hard to believe that the now-smooth water had been so dangerously violent.

I was grateful to be alive to hear the boatswain's tin whistle pierce the air and call all hands to muster on the *Esperance's* hangar deck, although despondent about Sweeney having been killed on lookout 3. Even the unfortunate crew members who were badly bruised and cut were overjoyed to be alive. I nursed a hatred of the OD on Sweeney's account, and berated myself for not having gone against orders sooner while Sweeney and I retained communication. I might've saved my friend's life! Now, the OD was probably sweeping the calm waters with his binoculars in search of survivors from ships that hadn't been as fortunate as the Esperance.

Steel ladders rattled as the last few sailors leaped two and three rungs at a time to reach the hangar deck. I couldn't believe my eyes when I spotted Sweeney's smile, same as ever. I broke ranks, ran over, and grabbed him.

"Sweeney, you sad sack of Iowa corn! For crying out loud, how did you escape?" I was practically crying with a combination of relief, joy, and disbelief.

He grinned. "Hey, man; no strain. Once I got scared enough, I figured I ain't gonna take a swim for that so-and-so OD. What's a little Bad Conduct Discharge with no mustering-out pay compared to making it back alive to good ol' Iowa with my sea bag? I watched those loose planes like a hawk, and at every bad list to starboard, I jumped into the light-lock [double doors to prevent lights shining outside]. When I saw the planes were gonna drop right on top of me, I jerked off my phones and jumped inside the light-lock."

"Man, did I ever regret that I didn't tell you, 'Permission granted' the first time you requested it, no matter what the OD said. He was delirious with fear, and not making any sense."

"Hey, there's Odenbaugh," Sweeney noted. "Stanley, where did you spend the roller coaster ride? You don't even look worried."

"I wasn't on watch, so I shouldered my accordion, strapped myself to a stanchion, and squeezed out tunes for all the cry babies below deck. Some of the foulest-mouthed guys you ever knew were worried about God all of a sudden, and searching for something interesting in the Bibles they had hid all this time."

I listened silently, knowing I was among their number, worrying about death and wondering about God.

During that morning's muster, all hands were accounted for, including men badly injured and lying in sick bay, unable to muster. The Skipper and Exec praised the seaworthiness of our good ship *USS Cape Esperance*, while the shipmates bragged about the great ship they served aboard. No one ever dared to refer to the ship as a

Sister ships show damage after the storm

"Kaiser's Coffin" any more.

With the unit in a state of disrepair, the *Esperance* limped into Guam for overnight mooring. We sailors unloaded the six airplanes in flying condition and choked down a few warm beers. We learned some of the reasons our ship didn't capsize and sink. All but six of the thirty-two planes we carried had been swept into the sea, which significantly altered the *Esperance's* center of gravity. Our load of block-buster bombs stored below the waterline provided sufficient ballast without overloading the ship. While the ordeal had been hair-raising, the loss of those heavy planes was a blessing in disguise. From officers to enlisted men were puzzled over how the ship's boom, the size of a telephone pole, made from inch-thick steel, had gotten twisted and bent. The crew of the good ship *Cape Esperance*, having lived through the most violent ocean storm on record, never forgot the shipwreck of three destroyers and the loss of nearly 800 men..

Early on the morning of June 5, 1945, yet another vicious typhoon, appropriately named Viper, smashed head-long into the Third Fleet with 120-knot winds. Still haunted by the fear of death and worried about my sinfulness, I didn't relax during the big blow.

Eight foot steel girders supported the forward ends of flight decks on aircraft carriers *USS Hornet* and *USS Bennington*. Those girders were so powerfully buffeted that they snapped, collapsing the forward decks on both ships. Possibly a defect in the construction of heavy cruiser *USS Pittsburgh* came to light during the thrashing and twisting it received from Typhoon Viper, 6 months after Typhoon Cobra. The immeasurable force of the storm tore off 104 feet of the cruiser's bow. With forward hatches tightly secured, the *Pittsburgh* remained afloat and navigable, while Navy sea tug *Munsee* towed her bow, amazingly still afloat, 950 miles to Guam.

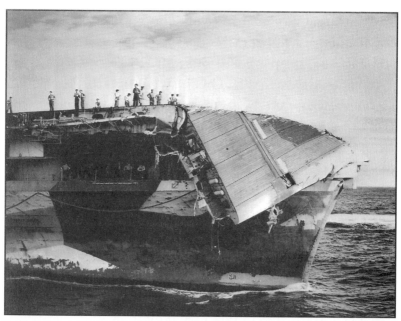

USS Bennington and USS Hornet shows deck damage after Typhoon Viper

All severely damaged ships remained afloat, although a few had been close to shipwreck. Every sailor on board was jubilant as the crippled *Esperance* sailed toward San Francisco for repairs. The first leg to Hawaii was smooth.

We picked up mail, which included an encouraging letter for me from my sister-in-law, Fran. Brother John, an Air Force bombardier assigned to a B-17, had his right hand and forearm torn open by shrapnel in the skies over Germany. The wounds resulted in complicated surgery to get his arm wired up for use. He and Fran were now stationed close to a hospital in the Bay area while he underwent extensive reconstructive surgery on his arm.

"Paul, as soon as you arrive in San Francisco, let us know and we'll make arrangements to get together," Fran's letter promised.

Since I was a smoker but not much of a drinker, some of the boys in the Second Division begged me to go with them on liberty and make sure they got back to the ship on time. "Come with us Slennah and we'll do the town up proper," they urged. "These people ain't got no idea how real sailors spend their pitiful pay and precious time. We'll pay for the taxis!"

That clinched it. My buddies and I had just one night to tear around Honolulu. Sweeney and I succeeded in getting the gang of bleary-eyed, vomit-stained swab jockeys crammed into a couple of taxis. One inebriant caused the taxi to wait while he leaned against a street lamp and wet his pants, giving his G.I.-issue shoes a sparkling shine that made them look like patent leather. I laughed with the others, but this experience disgusted me. I was every bit as rotten as the men who got drunk and raised hell that night. In fact, I might've joined them but for my fear of making it even harder to gain God's approval.

USS Pittsburgh under sail with part of bow missing.

Clean-up after the typhoon

Underway from Hawaii to the mainland, shipmate Craig got an even worse scare than our buddy Eldon had suffered. After noon chow one day, four of us leaned on the waist-high guard chains of the aft starboard sponson [a narrow side porch at hangar deck level] smoking Lucky Strikes and shooting the breeze. The water was a little choppy, with waves of eight to fifteen feet high, but smooth compared to what we had just survived. Out of nowhere, a freak wave slapped the hull close to, and higher than the sponson. The water jumped up, curved around toward us, and snatched Craig and George from between Kenny and me as though they were sticks of wood. George quickly snatched the guard chain with one hand, and pulled himself back on board. But Craig missed his reach for the chain by mere inches, and was tossed into the sea, drifting away as the ship sailed at about seventeen knots.

Swirling wave crests tumbled him first toward the ship, then away from it. We three lucky "shark baits" stood on the sponson, feeling fortunate not to be swimming to our deaths with Craig. Stricken with guilt as we watched Craig drift away, we were convinced he would never make it. A ship the size of a baby flattop—all 10,000 tons of her—can't just slam on its brakes and back up. It takes a long stretch of water in reverse gear for the behemoth to stop. The helmsman gave a hard right rudder to avoid drifting farther from Craig. Was the sea too rough to control a lifeboat? In hindsight, it seems that our only lack was modern rescue equipment with trained personnel.

Within minutes, Craig would either drown, or be ripped to shreds by scavenging sharks. He had removed his cumbersome jeans and shoes to facilitate swimming, but his white skivvies shone like a light in the water, attracting hungry sharks.

Five startling blasts from the ship's whistle announced, "Man overboard!" In less than a minute, the *Esperance's* engines shifted into neutral and then reverse. The Exec immediately grabbed the ship's bullhorn and shouted in a deafening roar, "For God's sake, don't swim son. Take your clothes off and just float! We'll come and git ya."

As if he didn't hear the bullhorn, Craig kept swimming. He finally spotted the life ring thrown to him, and just managed to reach it. The ship came as close as possible to the boy with its props in neutral to avoid sucking him into the enormous propellers. A cargo net was dropped over on the side where the close-to-being-done-for sailor was headed. Without an ounce of strength remaining, Craig was unable to hold onto the cargo net, let alone climb it.

Seaman Mong, a Pennsylvania Dutchman, aged 19, volunteered to climb down the cargo net to rescue the wild-eyed Craig. Mong's very appearance communicated great strength: thick, muscular legs supported a powerful torso that boasted arms the size of picnic hams. Mong descended the cargo net with dexterity. Waist-deep in the water, he held himself at arm's length from the *Esperance* so as not to be pounded against the steel hull. Gauging the distance and Craig's flagging strength, Mong shoved himself from the cargo net with a powerful thrust, swam the 30 yards to Craig, and towed his sinking shipmate back to the net.

Mong kept up a running patter to encourage Craig's waning strength as the tired man coughed and choked. "Hey, Craig, relax. We're doin' fine! Made in the shade is what we got. We're gonna slither up that net like gorillas. They'll give you a few swigs of torpedo juice as soon as we set foot on board, and get some heat in your bones. That'll put you back in business."

Mong seized the net with his right hand, and found footing for his bare feet. With his left arm wrapped around the kid's chest under each arm, he powered himself up the cargo net as if by inner hydraulics. Mong toted Craig to the top of the cargo net as though 135 pounds was no more trouble than a bag of marshmallows. Small as Craig was, he had remained afloat for twenty-seven minutes in rough water without a life jacket. For all his heroic efforts, Mong never received a promotion or recognition of any kind from any officer.

The first sight of the Golden Gate Bridge brought cheers from the crew that had escaped the vicious clutches of Typhoon Cobra (December 18, 1944) and Typhoon Viper (June 5, 1945). Men hugged each other and danced the jitterbug to the strains of loud jazz piped from the pier. Bottles of contraband whiskey appeared like magic and were passed for surreptitious swigs to celebrate being alive and in the good old U.S.A. It was torture to wait while the Esperance throttled back to let several whales leisurely paddle past our bow, before we could ease under the famous bridge to drop anchor in San Francisco Bay.

"All hands, mail call! All hands, mail call!" The alert from the Esperance's PA system triggered a stampede toward the approaching yeoman. The poor guy struggled to climb onto something high enough to avoid being trampled. A couple of dozen letters for me, most with Bonners Ferry return addresses, made my pulse quicken. More than a dozen came from Jessie, whose clear, melodious voice rang in my head as I read her letters.

On my last leave at home before shipping out, Jessie sang cowboy western songs as we rode along to nowhere particular in her sister's car. "I'm gonna drink my java from an old tin can when the moon is ridin' high...," she crooned. "Oh, that strawberry roan, he bucked me so high I thought I would die...There's a new moon over my shoulder and a new love down in my heart..." I could picture her smile even now, and hoped for ten days' leave while the *Esperance* was being repaired.

Alas! I was required to remain on duty during the *Es*-

perance's brief repairs, and only managed to see John and Fran the day before shipping back out to sea.

10

"Master, the tempest is raging, the billows are tossing high,
The sky is o'er-shadowed with blackness, no shelter or help is nigh.. ..
Carest Thou not if we perish?" came the anguished cry . . .
"Peace! Peace, be still. And know your Lord and Master's will." . . .
"What manner of Man is this, that the wind and waves obey Him?
'Tis Jesus, the wonderful Jesus! Who hath power to conquer the sea with its strife,
And whosoever believeth in Him shall not perish, but have everlasting life."
~Mary Ann Baker, 1874

The day before my scheduled sail, I deodorized myself
from cigarette smoke as much as possible with bay rum,
after shave, talcum powder, and mint gum. Then I threw
away my pack of smokes. All this was in preparation for
my meeting with John and Fran. If they knew I smoked, I
was sure they would give me a dose of fire and brimstone
from the Holy Bible.

My brother and sister-in-law pulled up to a waterfront
hotel in their 1932 Ford. Dad had caught a bus from Bonners Ferry to San Francisco for his first vacation since

moving to Idaho from South Dakota in 1936, nine years earlier. The hotel served as a meeting place, from which we headed to a restaurant for our evening meal. Our families were the main topic of discussion although, of course, John and I traded war stories. Fran asked me about Jessie, whom I admitted was the finest little lady I had ever met.

As we slid out of the booth, John said, "Hey, Paul, this is Sunday night. Fran and I have attended a real friendly church just a couple of blocks from here. Why don't you come with us to the evening service? There's still time to make it before it starts."

I looked down at the floor and then replied, "John, this might surprise you, but I can't wait to get there! I'll tell you, it's Fran's and your letters that made me think. God dangled me over hell when the *Esperance* sailed through Typhoon Cobra and then the one a few days ago (Viper) which also scared the ever-living daylights out of me. I didn't expect ever to set foot on dry ground again. I really don't want to return to sea tomorrow; I guess I'm a 160-pound chicken."

Being a bit late for the service, our little group grabbed seats on a back pew. The music was both lively and loud, and the pastor held my attention from his first words. I glanced at Dad, smiling as I remembered how he used to poke his finger between my ribs when I was stricken with uncontrollable giggles in Bonners Ferry's Methodist Church. I caused both Dad and Mom grave concern as a teenager, coming in late at night after tearing around with kids equally ornery and rebellious, and later running away from home.

Near the close of the service, the preacher stepped down from his pulpit. He said, "If there should be someone here tonight, civilian or military, who would like to enter into a right standing with God by receiving Christ as your personal Savior, please come down front so I can speak with you personally. It isn't necessary, but it would be my privilege to speak with you, to look into the Scriptures, and to pray with you. How wonderful if you would accept the Lord Jesus Christ as your personal Savior, and leave church tonight knowing that your sins are forgiven and you are saved for eternity! Many of you are on your way back to sea again; some of you are shipping out for the first time; others of you are headed to the battlefield. Don't go alone," he pleaded. "Take the Lord with you. He said of His children, 'I will never leave you nor forsake you.'"

That's what I wanted. I stood immediately, walked to the front of the auditorium, and knelt. No one asked me to kneel, and honestly, I'm not sure why I did other than a sense of awe and respect for God. One of the men from the church knelt besides me, put his arm around my shoulders, and said, "Glad to see you here, sailor." I burst into tears. I didn't know why I did that, either. This was a happy occasion! Yes, I was sorry for the sins I'd committed, but at the same time was overjoyed to be forgiven of them.

In little more than a whisper, the man said, "Sailor friend, you don't have to make this difficult. You heard tonight that Jesus Christ died on a cross to pay for your sins. He took your punishment for you. There is nothing you can do to save yourself. Simply believe that the Word of God is true, and accept Christ's atoning death for your salvation. If you really believe that with all your heart, tell God in a simple prayer right now that you accept Jesus Christ as your very own personal Savior.

My letter to Mom and Dad of July 1, 1945, briefly relates my experience the evening just a week earlier: "First, I want to tell you what a good time I had on that liberty with Dad, Johnny and Fran. I consider it the most important liberty I have ever taken. I suppose Dad is home by now and has told you, Mom, that we went to church that night in San Francisco. It was a real nice church with a large choir and an orchestra. That was the night I made a real decision for Christ. I thought it would be hard to go up in front of that huge congregation, but as I started toward the front, I didn't even realize that there was any congregation at all! When I left the altar, the church was almost empty. Several people came up and prayed with me for a while, then left again. Mr. Keys was the preacher; probably the best I have ever heard."

John, Fran, and Dad waited for me at the back of the auditorium, all smiles. We camped out that night on damp ground, with one blanket underneath us and one on top of us. It wasn't the last word in comfort, but it allowed us to spend more time together. The following morning after breakfast, John drove me to the dock where good ol' CVE 88 was moored. We hugged in fond farewell.

"We'll be praying for you," he told me. "Don't forget to read your Bible every day, and pray." I walked up the gangplank with a brand-new feeling about returning to sea. What happened at the church service on June 25, 1945, was the great turning point in my life. I have never been the same since then, but my spiritual growth as a new Christian was pitifully slow. I shared details about my new life in Christ with co-workers in the Exec's office, Damage Control office, and my closest friends on ship. Apparently, none of them had ever been converted. They listened to my account, shrugged, and then said, "Hmmm." Or, "Is that right?" Then they watched me like hawks to see if I would quit smoking, swearing, and carrying on like they were used to me doing.

V-J Day on August 15, 1945, that brought the official

end to World War II, occurred while the *Esperance* was cutting the brine at a poky 17 knots, returning to the U.S. from Guam. In Honolulu, I mailed a letter to Jessie Mac-Donald, describing Typhoon Cobra in blow-by-blow detail; telling about my meeting with John and Fran and Dad in San Francisco; and then sharing the news that I had become a Christian by accepting the Lord Jesus Christ as my personal Savior. "Jessie, I'm not sure how this will hit you," I wrote, "but my attitude about life in general is totally different. My life needs to be cleaned up and overhauled, so I'll be looking for a Bible-believing church to attend as soon as I'm discharged from the Navy."

I didn't know if I would ever hear from her again, or possibly a better-not-see-each-other-again letter. But I was encouraged by Jessie's response. "I think it's pretty good to be a Christian," she said. "I used to go to Sunday School in the Grange Hall at Three Mile. In fact, I once taught a lesson to the kids."

*   *   *

Under the Golden Gate Bridge again—this time, without whale delays—the *Esperance* made a straight shot to the shipyards for a lengthy day. The hangar deck would be fitted with bunks, four high, to convert her to a troop transporter. A number of sister ships underwent the same surgery to form a special fleet known as "The Magic Carpet", bringing soldiers from the war zone back to the U.S.

On this brief leave, I rode the train to Spokane, then caught a Greyhound bus the remaining 100 miles home to Bonners Ferry. Once in town, I walked up the aisle to ask the bus driver if he would drop me off at the intersection that led to my parents' home. "It's a small white house with green shutters and window boxes filled with petunias," I told him.

"Sure as shootin', son. Say, I bet you're glad the war is

over! Have a great time at home."

Mom was at home. Freshly laundered clothes just in from the line filled the davenport. "Oh, Pauly Lou, the war is over. Thank God you came home alive!"

"Yesiree, Mom. I'm glad to be back, even though I can't stay long. Gotta go back and bring home all the dog faces and bell hops (nicknames we sailors gave to members of other branches of the Armed Forces. They had plenty of nicknames for us, too.) I've been reading the Bible you gave me at Astoria. I'll tell you about it later, but right now, I need one full minute in your fridge."

Funny how delicious a stale piece of apple pie tastes! Dad brought home high-test cream from his commercial cream station, so thick it couldn't be poured after only a half-hour in the refrigerator. A spatula dab of that on a generous wedge of pie gave a restless sailor a new lease on life, back in the days before we knew about cholesterol.

I stomped up to my attic room, two steps at a time, thumped my snare drum, and tossed my sea bag onto my hard old bed. In San Diego, I'd had my dress blue trousers spiked and belled, and my shirt tailored to fit. A spit-shine on my black shoes elevated them to patent leather gloss, and with my white hat pressed down over my left eyebrow, I was ready for the mile-long walk into the center of my hometown.

Before the door had even shut behind me at the Fountain Café entrance, I spotted Jessie on duty, bright as a new silver dollar. Her light blue waitress's uniform, with an order pad in the apron pocket, set off her trim figure perfectly. The eraser end of a pencil protruded from her dark, wavy hair which bounced as she scurried from a booth to the kitchen, relaying an order. I could hardly wait to see her winning smile and big brown eyes, but I was also slightly fearful, not knowing what to say.

I swaggered to the last booth where the waitresses sat while they were still on shift. Bus drivers strategically stationed themselves in this booth for a wide-angle view of the comings and goings of the friendly staff. I well knew which waitress received the most attention!

A handsome bus driver, around 30, slumped in the roomy booth, elbows on the table to steady the hand that kept his weary head from drooping. His other hand, hooked onto a cup of coffee, held a cigarette between two fingers. As I approached, he took a long drag on his cigarette and pulled the smoke into the depths of his lungs. Twin streams of smoke poured from his nostrils to each side of his mug as he took another swig of coffee.

"Room for one more?" I asked, surprising myself that I found the courage to speak. But I wanted to occupy his strategic location myself, so my desperation summoned hidden reserves.

"Heck, yeah. Sit down, sailor; take a load off. How about a cup of freshly brewed stimulant?" he offered.

The bus driver's vocabulary proved colorful, to put it mildly, and despite my new-found faith, I had trouble not reverting to my old patterns of speech in response. When she saw me, Jessie came over to our booth with the coffee pot and a big smile for me.

"Took me by surprise, eh? When did you arrive?" Jessie inquired. Whew! I didn't have to worry about what to say, just answer her questions.

"Must've been on the bus that pulled in just before my new friend arrived," I quipped, indicating the bus driver.

Jessie performed the introductions. "Paul, this is Charlie, a regular customer here at the Fountain. Charlie, meet Paul, the guy I've been telling you about. Paul's nickname among the kids here in town is Slick Schlener; not sure how that got started or just what it means," she admitted.

I hoped it sounded like I was a bad hombre, not to be trifled with, as I exchanged nods and a hearty handshake with Charlie. A call to pick up an order summoned Jessie from the booth.

"Cute little gal, that Jessie," Charlie noted. "Have a cig with your coffee. Chesterfields okay?"

"Thanks, Charlie, I've been trying to quit and don't even have a match on me. And yes, indeed, with regard to our waitress. I've kept in touch with her since high school days, but I've been off getting salty so haven't been home lately to tend to business. I don't have her hobbled yet, but I'm working on it."

Charlie assured me, "Jessie speaks well of you. I doubt if you have to worry about anyone moving in on you."

Jessie floated by with another armload of plates and a sober glance for me, smoking with Charlie. When her normally smiling face switched to serious, it was alarming. As I walked her home from work, I learned why Jessie was disappointed in me. She had shared with everyone she knew that I had become a Christian, and didn't smoke, drink or cuss. And there I sat, smoking with Charlie, contributing an occasional low class adjective to the conversation.

"When you left the café to go see your dad until I got off work, Charlie called me over to the booth and said, 'Hey, how about Puritan Paul accepting the cigarette I offered him? Better check the lad a little closer!' I was embarrassed and didn't know what to say," Jessie scolded.

I knew she was right, and resolved to pay closer attention to the reputation I gave to my new-found faith. I saw Jessie at every opportunity during those few days of leave. Everything about her was perfect, as far as I was concerned. Jessie told me she thought she might be a Christian: her mom owned a Bible, and the MacDonald family occasionally attended church. I had met Jessie's 10 siblings: brothers and sisters, the sisters and their mom all shorter than Jessie's 5'-2". I intended to stay on the good side of her 6'-0" brothers. Since none of them seemed too concerned about the hereafter, I didn't intend to upset them by bringing up the subject.

All too quickly, it was time for me to head back to San Francisco and out to sea again. I wanted to remain in Bonners Ferry, ashore without leave. The war was over, but it would be months before I was released from active duty, since the Cape Esperance would be shuttling troops back home from overseas.

I never imagined myself thanking God for the typhoons that forced me to seek a relationship with Him by receiving the Lord Jesus Christ as my personal Savior, but that's exactly what I did! I was thrilled to know that my sins were forgiven because of Christ's death on the cross in my place. By shedding His blood, He paid the penalty for my sin and "purchased" my peace with God.

During the monotonous troop transport trips, I wondered what I ought to do with my life after the Navy. All I knew about the Bible was that it contained Old and New Testaments, although I didn't really even know what that meant. I just happened to notice a blank page dividing the two. I needed to find a good church someplace, and I needed to figure out what to do about Jessie. I couldn't forget her!

Letters from John and Fran kept me informed as to what they were doing. John was out of the Air Force now, and they lived on Bainbridge Island in the Puget Sound, where John worked as a painter in the ship yards.

"Lots of work here, Paul," he wrote. "When you get rid of your bellbottoms and scrape off all that salt, you'll find work here. You can stay with us."

*　　*　　*

As the *Esperance* pulled into San Francisco for what I hoped would be my final voyage, a USO band on the dock burst into lively music. Not since Samoa had a band welcomed the Esperance into port. My Navy career began and ended with band music, with lots of rough stuff thrown between them.

About a half-acre of the dock was covered with attractive young ladies, singing and throwing kisses to the goggle-eyed men on ship. An ocean of soft drinks and tons of donuts awaited the men leaving ship. Weary veterans, returning from the battlefields, crowded the port side of both hangar and flight decks to get a good look at the USO girls and inhale American air. Their weight caused the ship to lean at an angle that reminded us sailors of the typhoons that nearly upended us.

From San Francisco, the *Esperance* chugged up to the port of Bremerton, Washington, where those in charge waited in the Separation Center to release most of the Esperance's crew before the ship herself headed to Mukleteo to be mothballed. What a relief it was to walk the plank for the last time, never to return to sea aboard the *USS Cape Esperance*!

When John and Fran learned of my approximate discharge date from the Navy, they immediately invited Jessie to visit them in Bainbridge Island. She was between jobs with nothing to prevent her from accepting their invitation—except, perhaps, her mom.

"What do you want to go to Seattle for?" Mrs. MacDonald demanded. "There's no need for you to go traipsing off all alone like that. And how well do you know this Slick Schlener anyway?"

Jessie sold her mom on John and Fran's integrity, explaining that they were Christian people with whom she would stay in their apartment. John would even meet her at the train, Jessie said.

And did John ever meet her! He gloated over the experience decades later. When petite, sparkling Jessie stepped out of the passenger car, the air filled with what sounded like the piccolo section of an orchestra. Wolf whistles, oohs, and ahs were emitted as John escorted Jessie past a crowd of swab jockeys, waiting for trains to their homes. John acted like her owner, wearing a big grin as he attempted to stretch himself higher than his actual five feet, eight inches.

My discharge at the separation center in Bremerton was held up, but John and Fran entertained Jessie royally. Their friends were mainly church people, which meant that Jessie was taken to church. A lot! She enjoyed the ferryboat rides to Seattle from the island, and seeing the big city itself. But good grief! Only going to church? Saturday night was the youth rally at church, where quartets, trumpet trios, and personal testimonies were all given by young people. Jessie had never heard or seen anything like it.

Early the next morning found them leaning on the ferryboat's guard rails once again as they sailed toward Tabernacle Baptist Church on Capitol Hill in Seattle. The worship service lasted more than an hour, by Jessie's reckoning, with the pastor's message aimed straight at her— or so it seemed to her.

That Sunday was the first Sunday of the month, which happened to coincide with the church's celebration of the Lord's Supper. This involved reading appropriate passages from the Bible, prayer, and ended with eating a small piece of bread and drinking a miniature tumbler full of grape juice. A lady sitting next to her whispered to Jessie,

"This is all new to you. Don't worry or be embarrassed; simply pass the plates on to the next person." Even still, Jessie was slightly embarrassed by the whole thing.

John and Fran and their son, little John, were invited to their friends' house after church, and were instructed to "be sure and bring Jessie". After the meal, the family and guests gathered around a piano and sang. Jessie was a good country western singer and yodeler, but hymns weren't down her alley. She stood with the group for a few minutes, listening, and then excused herself. She slipped into a bedroom and began weeping when Mary Roberts, the lady of the house, found her. "Jessie, honey, what seems to be the trouble?" she asked. "Are you a little homesick, maybe?"

"I don't know, Mrs. Roberts. Everyone is nice to me. I enjoyed the delicious dinner, but I feel out of place. I just don't belong here with these people!" Jessie sobbed.

Mrs. Roberts hastened to reassure the young woman. "These young people are glad you're here. Several have remarked how nice you are, and I noticed some of the boys trying to get your attention. Come on, let's have a cup of coffee and then we'll go back out there and sing with the gang."

Jessie hit it off well with the Roberts. Idris, Mary's husband, was a journeyman plumber of Scottish descent, put him in good with Jessie MacDonald. Idris was also an amateur photographer.

"Come over here, girls. Yes, you, Jessie and Fran. I want my picture taken with the two fanciest ladies in King County." They giggled and demurred, but with Fran on one knee and Jessie on the other, Idris posed for a snapshot.

A few hours later they were off to church again for the evening service, with the preacher once again focused on

Jessie. It was a relief to her when she and the Schleners boarded the ferry back to Bainbridge Island. By that point, Jessie later admitted, she was anxious for my arrival. And I arrived the very next day, swinging my bellbottoms with my "ruptured duck" [emblem issued at the time of discharge from the Navy) on my left shoulder, my white sea bag, and $300 mustering-out pay burning a hole in my pocket.

That same dark, rainy night, Jessie and I, together with John and Fran and little John, headed to the Roberts home which had become a kind of hangout for Christian military personnel. About half-way across the bridge, we noticed a man standing on the crosswalk, one foot on the bottom rail and both hands on the top rail, as he pushed and pulled himself back and forth. His car was parked in the passing lane, blocking traffic. We quickly concluded that he was about to attempt suicide by jumping over the railing. John slammed on his brakes, and he and I flew out of the car. We vaulted over the rail that separated automotive traffic from the pedestrian lane, and seized the man who never noticed us until we were at his side. Our ladies didn't appreciate being left in busy traffic at risk of receiving lectures or tickets from traffic cops.

The 27-year-old man sobbed as he struggled to free himself from John's and my grasp. "Don't try to stop me, you damn fools, or you'll get hurt. I just want to get this over with now." Our plan to secure him was cemented with imperceptible nods. I grabbed his legs in a standing tackle, while John grabbed his shoulders and pulled him to the deck. The poor guy realized we had him pinned; seeing the gathered crowd and hearing the shrieking sirens, he slowly relaxed. The police's arrival relieved John and me of our struggle.

"Nice going, fellows," an officer said. "Call this number

tomorrow and I'll let you know where this guy will be held, if you should want to visit him. You might bring the poor man some cheer, pull him out of the doldrums."

The next day, John and I found the man totally despondent, but appreciative that we had stopped him from ending his life. When we spotted him on the bridge, the poor man had just received word from his doctors that he was afflicted with a terminal illness. On his way home, he was overwhelmed with hopelessness and unable to face giving his wife and three children the bad news. During our brief conversation with the man, John led him to a saving knowledge of the Lord Jesus Christ.

That sobering experience reminded all of us that we don't know what is around the next corner of our lives. We need to be prepared to stand before God at any moment, because we never know when this life will come to an end.

*　　*　　*

Jessie and I lost no time in finding ways to catch the ferry to Seattle for activities other than church. My first stop was a department store to buy civilian clothes, which Jessie helped me choose. Boy, was I ever proud to have an attractive girlfriend helping me! I took a dim view of other men giving her a second glance, but I understood their envy.

Bus rides around town and lunch at the Pike Place Market left us just enough time to ferry back to Bainbridge Island for Fran's evening meal. But April 6, 1946 wasn't over yet; the best was yet to come—very late that night.

"John, how about loaning me your jitney?" I asked. "I feel the need to take 'little Mac' for a spin around the island."

"Help yourself," he responded. "The tank's full. But you'd better put on your sailor suit so you don't get a ticket for driving without a license." My big brother was always ready with advice for little brother, Paul. His machine was a 1937 Ford with mechanical brakes, one of the first flathead V8 engines ever built, and it could scamper like a whippet.

By the time I mustered up my courage, it was already 9:00 p.m. John and Fran might've wondered why Jessie and I got such a late start and what we were up to, but since they enjoyed their own courting days—some of which I personally witnessed—they might've had an idea as to my plans. But I don't think they knew exactly what I had in mind.

I had worried for a long time about how to talk to my sweetheart about becoming a Christian. What time I spent talking to girls in high school was a total wash-out, probably for lack of accomplishment on my part and certainly nothing to recall with any pride. Jessie was easy to talk to, her voice clear and full of expression, pitched a bit lower than the average female squeak. But the subject I intended to approach could very well squelch her easy-going, cheerful temperament.

Pausing for a milkshake, I took another street to its end, killing time. I was just too chicken to broach the subject. Finally, I parked halfway between the city block streetlights so that we were sitting in almost total darkness. *Now*, I told myself. *Oh, God, give me the right words to say and don't let me say the wrong thing!*

I began, "Jessie, I don't know how to explain to you what I'm thinking." Bang! I was struck with almost as much panic as I had suffered on the *Esperance's* open bridge during typhoon Cobra. But I stammered on. "I want you to know I have never felt about any girl like I do about you. I'm sure I love you, and if you should ever have the same feeling, we might want to get married. Serious problems could result if we should marry while we don't believe the same thing about God." Having uttered those fateful words, my vocal chords, tongue and lips immediately succumbed to paralysis. The only thing I knew anything about was life as a sailor. Now what?

I eventually managed to find my voice. "You know what happened to me out at sea, and how I accepted the Lord Jesus Christ as my personal Savior at the church in San Francisco." Jessie nodded, as if I'd made sense so far. "I know I'm not the Christian I should be. I don't know much about the Bible yet, but it seems like we should see eye to eye and heart to heart about being Christians and about church attendance before we get too involved with each other. What do you think?"

Jessie didn't answer. That minute of silence seemed to last an hour, and I was struck with discouragement. I had botched it, completely fumbled the ball! Why did I have to be in such an all-fired hurry? Mentally chastising myself, I reached for the starter. A little sniffle made me glance at Jessie the very moment a tear from one of her big, brown eyes rolled down her cheek. It sparkled from the light a half block away. She removed a hanky from her purse to mop her tears. It's all over, I thought as she cleared her voice to speak.

"Paul," she began, a slight quiver in her voice. I waited, worried, until she went on in a clearer tone. "I don't know what to say except that ... I would like to be like those people gathered in the Roberts' home after church. I have never heard young people sing and talk like they did at the youth rally. Seems like Pastor Johnson was speaking to me, personally on Sunday, and I know I need what he was talking about."

Boy, did Jessie ever have my full attention now. Between sniffles she said, "John and Fran have been so good to me! I'd like to be like them. If you call that being a Christian or being saved, that's what I would like."

I suffered an attack of goose bumps, immediately followed by an overwhelming relief that Jessie made the decision she did. "Hang on!" I told her. I started the old Ford and laid a strip of rubber on the pavement as I hot-footed it back to John and Fran's apartment. I made a wrong turn and ended up facing the Puget Sound. I backed up, all excited, and took another route, only to run into the shoreline yet again. Lost like never before, I was fast losing whatever confidence Jessie might have placed in me. I was glad John had topped off his gas tank, because it was way after midnight when Jessie and I finally reached the apartment.

I banged on the bedroom door and yelled, "Hey, guys! Can you come out here for a minute? We want to talk to you?" Groans and thumping heels on the bedroom floor greeted my loud voice. John shuffled out, hair mussed and squinting at his wristwatch. He splashed cold water on his face in the bathroom before facing us.

"Sorry to disturb you at this time of the night..."

"Night?? It's morning, sailor boy! What happened? Did you have to walk home? What's wrong with the car?" he demanded.

"We got lost," I mumbled sheepishly. "I kept running into water."

"How does a sailor manage to get lost on an island?"

A few minutes later, Fran joined us in the living room. I told them, "Jessie and I had a serious talk. She told me she wanted to be saved, to become a Christian. Frankly, I don't know exactly what to tell her other than that I'm overjoyed with her decision. John, get your Bible and tell her what she needs to hear. *You* know the verses!"

When Jessie received the Lord as her Savior during the

wee hours of that morning, there was great rejoicing. Tears of joy flooded our eyes as the four of us prayed together and hugged one another before turning in to sleep for the few remaining hours before daylight.

11

Eternal Father, strong to save, whose arm hath bound the restless wave,
Who bidd'st the mighty ocean deep its own appointed limits keep;
O hear us when we cry to Thee, for those in peril on the sea!

O Christ whose voice the waters heard and hushed their raging at Thy word,
Who walk-edst on the foaming deep, and calm amidst its rage didst sleep;
O hear us when we cry to Thee, for those in peril on the sea!

Most Holy Spirit who didst brood upon the chaos dark and rude,
And bid its angry tumult cease, and give, for wild confusion, peace;
O hear us when we cry to Thee, for those in peril on the sea!

O Trinity of love and pow'r, our brethren shield in danger's hour;
From rock and tempest, fire and foe, protect them wheresoe'er they go;
Thus evermore shall rise to Thee glad hymns of praise from land and sea.

~ "Sailor's Hymn" by William Whiting, 1860

Jessie's decision to trust Christ as Savior was headline news at Tabernacle Baptist Church, and the good news spread quickly. She was smothered in congratulations and promises to pray for her. Jessie was amazed at the way Christians demonstrated their love for her, while I kept an eye on some of the younger gentlemen who seemed to push the bounds of fellowship. But church now held new meaning for both of us.

While she loved her family greatly, Jessie sensed a need for more Bible teaching and Christian fellowship before returning home. Mary Johnson, the pastor's wife, approached Jessie one Sunday after church and asked if she would be willing to help out with care for the new baby they were expecting in a matter of days. "We would love to have you stay in our home" she assured Jessie.

Jessie accepted the invitation with a touch of reluctance, wondering what it would be like to live under the same roof with a reverend and his family. At least she would be able to study and fellowship the way she desired. During church services, Jessie and I were challenged to give our lives completely to the Lord, and be willing to do whatever God wanted us to. We were peppered with questions from Pastor Johnson: "Do you have any plans for the future? What are you going to do with your lives? Do you plan to continue your education?" Jessie and I looked at each other and shrugged, spreading our hands. Our response was something along the lines of, "Rev. Johnson, we hadn't ever thought about this, but thank you for challenging us to think about these important subjects."

Kathy, the Johnsons' new-born baby, brought the number of children in the family to four. Almost non-stop visitors— mostly missionaries to foreign countries and pastors of other churches—to the Johnson home kept Jessie and Mary running between the washing machine, ironing board, kitchen sink, and vacuum cleaner.

The children were always well-behaved and friendly. One evening when the house was bursting with guests, Mary whispered to Jessie, "Would you run upstairs and put the kids to bed for me? They might ask you to tell them a story or something."

Jessie readily agreed, following the kids as they scrambled up the stairs, appearing not in the least bit tired. But they donned their pajamas and jumped into bed. "Good night, see you in the morning," Jessie called, starting for the stairway.

"But, Jessie," they protested, "aren't you going to pray with us before we go to sleep? Mom always prays before she tucks us in."

This was a new one for Jessie. Before bed as a youngster, she was lucky to defend herself against four sisters sharing the room, never mind about praying!

"You know what, kids? I'm sorry but I don't really know how to pray. You say your prayers, and I'll learn from listening to you!"

One evening, the house was so full of guests, Mary told Jessie she was going to have a missionary lady as a bedmate for the evening. Although assured that the missionary was a wonderful Christian, Jessie wasn't keen on the idea of sharing her bed with anyone. She'd rather have slept in the garage or a chicken coop, and nearly fell off the bed trying to sleep as close to the edge as possible.

The next morning at breakfast time, Mary asked each of the guests how many eggs each of them would like, thinking "one or two?" A corpulent man, also a missionary to foreign lands, said, "I'll take four, over easy."

Mary, quick with clever repartee responded, "Sorry, brother. You'll have to take two over-easy, and I hope you will enjoy them both."

The evening I proposed to Jessie, we were sitting on the front porch of the parsonage while the Johnsons dined with friends. Along with a minuscule diamond engagement ring I had for Jessie, I should have slipped a magnifying glass into her purse so friends could see the tiny stone!

Paul and Jessie's engagement

*   *   *

We hadn't really learned to trust God to provide for all our needs. Jessie was employed at the Boundary County Courthouse in Bonners Ferry, while I was a spray-painter in the Seattle shipyards. It was discouraging for me as a young Christian to listen to profane speeches from union bosses during the union meetings. Perverse language had been one of my weaknesses as a sailor, but little by little as I socialized with other Christians, the Lord cleaned up my filthy talk.

While spraying zinc oxide in empty spaces below the

waterline on big ships back from war-time service, I was again challenged to seek God's will for my life. Equipped with ventilation masks at the end of a hundred-foot extension cord and air hose, a group of us took 15 minute turns with spray guns, shooting the poisonous mixture. Inhale too much of the fumes, and you pass out – sometimes, for good.

Moments after I started my fifteen minutes shift, or so it seemed, I felt a jerk on the line. Glancing back toward the entrance, I saw no one, so continued my spraying figuring that somebody must've tripped over the hose. Within what seemed a fraction of a minute, I felt another pull on the line and ignored what I knew to be my partners, pulling a prank on me. The next thing I saw was a guy coming toward me with a light, his face hidden behind a mask that gave him the appearance of a baby elephant.

He grabbed my arm and in his best union steward's profanity, hollered through his mask, "Drop that spray gun, you so-and-so, and get the heck out of here right this minute. Dagnabbit! You've been in here for better than half an hour."

"No way!" I yelled back. "I haven't been in here even ten minutes!" But I dutifully followed him out to the entrance. At the first breath of fresh air, my knees buckled. Two men dragged me over to a bench where I sat until my equilibrium returned. I decided that this was not the way I wanted to spend my life. But what did I want to do?

I quit the shipyard in July 1947, returning to Bonners Ferry. Jessie and I appreciated Pastor Johnson's advice to study for one year at a Bible institute before deciding on our lives' work. And since John and Fran were half-way through their first year at the Bible Institute of Los Angeles (BIOLA) when Jessie and I got engaged, we also applied to BIOLA for the one-year course, figuring that would give us the necessary instruction to live the way we should. We were fortunate to be accepted in the last year the school accepted applicants without a high school diploma.

I often wonder if any young couple ever got married with a smaller bank balance than Jessie and I had when we married. Before leaving Seattle, I had purchased a double-breasted grey sharkskin suit for my August 3 wedding to Jessie at the Methodist Church in Bonners Ferry. Young Rev. Walsh performed the ceremony, which I didn't hear one word of until he reached the main questions. My brother John, home from Los Angeles, was my best man; Jessie's younger sister, Ruth, was her bridesmaid.

My sister, Ruth Nuckols, a teacher and artist, decorated the church auditorium. Along with tons of flower arrangements, two winged doves in flight, holding ribbons in their beaks, were suspended from the ceiling above the platform. In an attempt to avoid eye contact with anyone in the congregation, I kept my focus on those doves, thinking, "Man, what an easy target with a sling shot!" Never having plumbed the depths of higher learning, I didn't recognize the symbolism represented by the doves: the Holy Spirit and peace.

Jessie's sister, Doris Howard, baked and decorated a beautiful cake; while the ladies of the church favored us by providing a scrumptious reception.

Pastor Walsh stood next to Jessie and me in the receiving line, puffing and dripping with sweat. He swabbed his face and neck with a handkerchief, loosened his tie, and removed his suit coat. As the congratulators formed a line, he shook my hand and kissed the bride, saying rapidly, "I certainly want to congratulate you fine folks and wish you happiness without end as you establish your new home.

But I have to admit to being scared half to death during the ceremony; had you been the king of one country and princess of another, I couldn't have felt more pressure."

We assured him of our gratitude for services rendered. "Had you stuttered, coughed, or even shed tears, we wouldn't have noticed it because WE were so nervous at standing in front of all those people!"

Jessie and I flew out the front door under a shower of rice, jumped into the Chevy, and high-tailed it to Priest Lake for a three-day honeymoon. Our transportation was a recently purchased 1936 Chevy sedan with front wheel king pins so worn, the wheels slanted like a knock-kneed county road grader. The previous owner admitted to not knowing when the sedan's odometer quit, but clearly it had burned up so many miles on pavement and rough Idaho graveled roads, that its longevity was nearly through. The inner tubed tires had just enough tread remaining to show that they once had tread. My tendency to worrying was not yet evident at 21 years of age; I didn't feel the least bit of concern about the possibility of a flat tire. In fact, changing a tire at that point in time would've allowed me to show my bride what a great mechanic she had married!

Perfect weather blessed us during those three days. The circa-1929 tourist cabins on the lake shore of what we consider basic necessities today: air conditioners, telephones, showers, microwave ovens, and television were not to be found. An outhouse at the end of a path leading from the back door served as our bathroom.

I made sure to bring important items for a honeymoon, such as my fishing tackle and a .22 rifle. We rented a small boat powered by a 2hp outboard engine that strained to push us even two miles an hour. We trolled while feasting our eyes on the wondrous North Idaho scenery. But when no strikes hit the line, listening to the whine of an engine grows boring.

A couple of days at Dad and Mom Schlener's gave Jessie and me time to pack our wedding presents and load them into a homemade auto-top carrier. The back seat, packed with stuff from floor to the bottom of the rear window, bogged us down for the ride to Los Angeles. We drove in a caravan with John and Fran to our new home. Neither the heavy load, the age of the car, or bald tires concerned me.

California or Bust! Paul and Jessie ready to leave with John R. Schlener looking on.

Things changed when we eased away from the great Northwest. The windows were rolled down to give us a breeze, torrid as it was. Day two on highway 99 in the State of California brought the threat from shreds of blown-out tires along the highway. Jessie and I grew concerned, wondering how long our bald tires would hold air. If even one of them popped, how would the top-heavy load trundling along at the break neck speed of 50 miles per hour avoid tipping us over? We didn't have a blowout or even a flat on the entire trip from Bonners Ferry to 222 West Ramona Boulevard, Wilmar, California! But the following morning the left rear tire was as flat as a phonograph record. Jessie and I were learning to trust God's providential care for His children as He led us along!

A veteran of first-year studies, John already had steady part-time employment as a painter on BIOLA's maintenance crew, which he recommended I join. Mr. Guthrie, coordinator of building maintenance, sounded as though he might be of Irish descent as he graciously welcomed me to his group of workers. Soiled striped overalls hung on his frail frame, with a watch fob dangling from the top pocket. His tiny, battered desk held a well-worn Bible perched atop cluttered papers, as though he had just finished reading a portion of it. A cursory glance around showed nothing orderly or brand new in Mr. Guthrie's diminutive, gloomy, work station.

Ancient subterranean pipes and tubes overhead and along walls gave proof that we were way below street level of sixth and Hope.

But the Christian man was never short-tempered or angry; he was simply a good guy to work for. Getting used to the Schlener brothers probably proved to be a challenge to him. We had the habit of trying to be amusing as we worked in the dusky passageways of the subterranean basement. While Mr. Guthrie was normally straight-faced and serious, he occasionally emitted a quiet, squeaky laugh.

My first assignment in BIOLA's maintenance department revived memories of my days standing on an open bridge aboard the *USS Cape Esperance* during the typhoons. The old thirteen-story Willard Hotel, a U-shaped building at Sixth and Hope Streets, housed the girls dormitory along the south leg of the U. Low-rent rooms for the elderly lined the north leg, and the Church of the Open Door (seating capacity: 3,000) was housed under the same massive roof.

Joe, one of the grinning Goodman brothers and a fellow first-year student, joined me as we scraped and repainted the building's exterior fire escapes. When the first landing on the top fire escape ladder was finished, the bottom side had to be attacked from underneath. A plank positioned on the guard rail across the corners of the second landing allowed me to reach the underside of the top landing.

People walking around on the main floor looked like midgets to us, perched so high aloft. Without a safety net or harness seat, I grabbed hold of the cross braces to reach the outside parts. Everything went well for a while as Joe and I hollered back and forth to each other, until a sudden gust of wind blew the worthless painter's cap off my head. Without thinking, I let go of the cross braces to snatch it. As I leaned out to grab it, I realized barely in time to catch myself from plunging twelve stories. That scared me so bad, I had to lay off for the rest of the day, unable to stand up straight or even peer over the scaffolding.

* * *

Dr. Louis Talbot was greatly used of God during his many years as the pastor of Church of the Open Door, whose stated mission was to spread the gospel of Jesus Christ to unsaved people throughout the world. Jessie and I found Dr. Talbot's accent amusing, as he was an American citizen from Australia. After one of his trips, he announced, "Oi sawr South Americker [I saw South America]."

On one occasion, as the deacons made their way down the aisles to the front of the auditorium to receive the morning offering, Pastor Talbot requested all men present to stand. He said, "I want to make it easier for you to reach the wallets in your rear pockets. Now for you ladies, it will be more convenient to remain seated to facilitate opening the heavily laden purses on your laps, while you retrieve a generous portion of the Lord's provision to you to contribute to this offering."

The vast crowd of men's elbows bended to reach into their pockets; it was equally funny to see hundreds of ladies, digging in their purses. My wallet held nothing more than a driver's license and a few photos, but I followed suit in reaching for my flat wallet. All Jessie could do was rummage in her handbag with an equal lack of result.

At another Sunday service, Pastor Talbot announced, "The ministry of music was wonderful this morning and included a beautiful offertory, but I notice that the plates are scantily filled. Ushers, am I right?" They all nodded in agreement. "That being the case, gentlemen, having already prayed for the offering, please pass the plates again while the organist and pianist encourage us to be generous as we give to the Lord." Glancing briefly at the instrumentalists, he asked, "Ladies, will you give us a lively rendition of *Bringing in the Sheaves*? We've got to get this sanctuary out of debt before the rapture takes place." The Church of the Open Door was debt-free before Pastor Talbot retired.

Property belonging to deceased church members was often bequeathed by will to BIOLA or to the church. These properties were refurbished and then sold. John and Fran, fortunate to receive disabled retirement pay from the Air Force, were in the process of purchasing one of those modest homes near the Los Angeles suburb of Rosemead. Jessie and I were the recipients of their generosity, and briefly occupied one of two bedrooms in their home. We enjoyed their hospitality for as long as it took the Grinning Goodman brothers to roughly finish the interior of John's single-car garage, which Jessie and I rented from him for $25 per month.

Paul (a.k.a., Bud), Bill, and Joe Goodman, all three handsome six-footers, were perfectly built for the building business they pursued - muscular and sturdy. They also were a musical trio, singing lively western ballads and gospel choruses while strumming their guitars. Joe, the youngest, yodeled like a pro as though he was a graduate of a Swiss Yodel academy.

Early one Saturday morning, the three guys screeched to a halt on John's driveway and poured out of their truck's cab as though prodded by an electric current. Each grabbed a pick, shovel, hoe, or cement trowel. Hammers and steel tape measures already hung from their tool belts. Taking long strides, they flashed broad grins at Jessie and me as we stood in front of the garage. Obviously, these men were full of energy and knew what they were about. Jessie and I immediately saw that the best thing we could do to enhance progress, was to stay out of the mens' way and let the men get right to their business.

Fran and Jessie kept frying pans sizzling and kettles bubbling for the noon meal, hoping they had sufficient grub to satisfy the hearty appetites of our volunteer workers. They finished the entire floor, mixing cement by hand and roughing in the plumbing, before their 3:00 p.m. coffee break. The only expertise I could offer while the men perspired and strained was to keep cold drinks within their reach.

The next Saturday morning, Jessie and I spied from John and Fran's kitchen window what appeared to be a parade of sheet rock slabs marching by and into the garage. With the swiftness of whirlwinds, the Grinning

Goodmans had the interior of our garage apartment finished in a couple of days, complete with plumbing, wiring, and even shiny linoleum laid on the floor.

God provided our every need, in ways we never anticipated. Two deep sinks served us newlyweds for both dishwashing and laundry. We purchased a hide-a-bed sofa which lasted during our four-year sojourn in California. It unfolded into a double bed, placing our feet mere inches from the oven of an ancient gas range. A plain oak icebox was good enough until someone gave us their old refrigerator with an exterior coil mounted on top. It worked, though, and was a great boon over the old icebox!

The Pacific electric train, consisting of two cars at the most, ran irregular hours both day and night, rumbling by a hundred fifty yards from our apartment. The roar soon blended into the background, and it was hard to fall asleep without that "soothing rumble". Often, we hummed the tune to *The Wabash Cannonball*: "Listen to the jingle, hear the rumble and roar as she glides along the woodland, meadow and shore..."

12

As freshmen at the great Bible Institute of Los Angeles, Jessie and I continued to learn how the Lord provides the needs of those who trust in Him. We find ourselves still enjoying how the Lord provides even after more than sixty years of marriage.

The faculty of BIOLA was a collection of some of the greatest Bible scholars in the nation, in my unbiased opinion. I'm sure they did their best to make the curriculum comprehensible to us. Dr. Bernard Ramm taught hermeneutics and Christian philosophy. The very first day of class in the first class of the morning, Dr. Ramm welcomed us and asked a simple, three-word question, "What is philosophy?"

He swept the classroom with a glance which—unluckily—stopped at my red plaid shirt. "You in the red shirt. Your name, please." I froze instantly, barely able to respond.

"What is philosophy? What does 'philosophy' mean?"

he repeated, nary a hint of humor on his face as he zeroed in on me.

I must have paled like a ghost, but after a giant swallow, I stammered, "Sir, this course is on my required list of studies [as if he didn't know that!], but I have to admit I can't explain what it means. I'm hoping to learn what it means during this semester."

He nodded.

Seeking to share their knowledge and certain they knew the definition Dr. Ramm sought, my humiliation prompted numerous students to wave their hands wildly, as though the correct answer would yield the lucky student a hundred dollar bill. However, many of their responses did not meet with success. And although I made sure never to wear my plaid shirt to class again, Dr. Ramm never called on me to answer a question for the remainder of the semester.

Occasionally during his lectures, he assumed an unblinking stare, focused on the floor of the aisle between the two groups of students not ten feet from his lectern. He indicated a page number of the textbook, and proceeded to recite the page as though he held the open book in his hands. I stretched my neck to see the floor where he was looking, wondering if he had a sheet of paper planted there with large enough print to be readable for him.

Rev. Padgette taught public speaking to first-year students. The class name was later changed to homiletics, which I called humble-etics. Green, yellow, and red lights in clear view put the brakes on long-winded speakers. I struggled to share some of my experiences at sea aboard the *USS Cape Esperance*. Standing in front of the class, I knew my hair was messed, my ears too big and my nose too long. I was equally sure that my pants bagged. I lasted 90 seconds before my vocal chords seized and I high-tailed it back to my seat. The red light never stood a chance!

When morning classes ended, I headed straight for Rev. Padgette's office. He politely asked what he could do for me as he shuffled papers on his desk.

"Not much, I'm afraid," was my response. "In fact, the reason I'm here is to ask you to remove my name from the list of students in public speaking class."

That got his attention. He looked up at me. "Mr. Schlener, what is your reason for quitting the class?"

"Professor Padgette, you just heard my performance a few minutes ago. I was done in less than two minutes and had to quit! I don't want to get up in front of the class again. I'm sure this course would be beneficial, but with all due respect to you, sir, I didn't enroll in the Bible Institute in order to preach in any way, shape, or form. I simply wanted to study the Bible! Can't I just do that?"

Rev. Padgette looked at me for a long moment. He stood, walked around his desk, and stood eye-to-eye with me, wearing a weak grin.

"Mr. Schlener, you did a good job this morning. You made a good appearance before the class [I'd worn a single-breasted suit and highly-shined shoes]; there is nothing for you to be ashamed of. The entire class is in the same boat. I didn't notice any silver-tongued orators here. The class will be disappointed if you don't finish the story you started." His meager grin grew into a broad smile. He shook my hand, adding, "I'm not going to remove your name from the class list. Just come to the next session and finish your story; you'll do fine."

I left Rev. Padgette's office with a definite spring in my step. But sleep that night was sporadic, since I didn't feel a miracle occur to transform the second half of my oration. By God's grace and wearing the same—my only—suit, I stammered all the way to the red light.

Dr. J. Vernon McGee's synthesis classes made the monotonous trips to downtown Los Angeles worthwhile. He became pastor of Church of the Open Door upon Pastor Talbot's retirement. He made the Old Testament come to life, admitting his weakness in pronunciation of Old Testament names, both locations and people. A distinguished scholar who graduated from Dallas Theological Seminary with high honors, Dr. McGee's homey illustrations delivered in a southern drawl held his students' attention. Our claim to fame on the paint crew was varnishing the wood-paneled den in his new home in Pasadena, although John and I were never privileged to become personally acquainted with the great man of God.

Dr. Charles L. Feinberg, ThD. and PhD. dean of Talbot Theological Seminary, taught the book of Revelation, Apologetics I, II, and III, as well as Archaeology and other courses geared to seminary students. A convert from Judaism, Dr. Feinberg was an amazingly humble man. He was one of eight scholars on the Editorial Revision Committee for the Scofield Study Bible, and authored numerous books.

In 1963, sixteen years after studying at BIOLA, Jessie and I were living in La Habra, California, and attending Hope Union Church where we held practical work assignments during our student days. Dr. Feinberg was the guest speaker at church that Sunday morning, and during the 15-minute period between Sunday school and morning services, I was parked on a back pew talking with one of the deacons while waiting for Jessie to return from the ladies' room.

As the deacon and I chatted, Dr. Feinberg and his son appeared. Both men glanced over the sanctuary and paused briefly before slowly walking toward us and stopping in front of us. I jumped to my feet, thinking a nod and a friendly "Good morning" was in order. But no, the great man held out his hand for me to shake.

"Hello, Paul," he said, nearly sending me into shock that he remembered my name. "How are things going down on the Amazon?"

I'm surprised that my knees didn't buckle on the spot. I have no idea what I said, so taken aback was I that he remembered my name from among the thousands of students he'd taught over the years. I'd never worn the red plaid shirt in Dr. Feinberg's class, nor had he ever called on me in class. The scholarly man was gracious to pass me with low marks in both archaeology and exegesis of Revelation. And since I hadn't seen him since BIOLA, how did he know Jessie and I had gone to Brazil the year after to minister along the Amazon River?

*　*　*

My courageous wife didn't have an easy time during our first year at BIOLA: living in a tiny garage apartment on a tiny income, and riding the electric train after classes while John and I raced across town in the wild LA traffic to a painting job. She never knew when I would get home from work in those pre-cell phone days. Often with nothing more than loose pocket change, Jessie and I often wondered where our next meal would come from. Jessie would start digging in her purse, which remains an amusing past-time to this day for me to watch. From there she moved to tossing clothes in the dresser drawers and peeking in cupboards. Finally, she would glide over to where I paced back and forth, displaying enough quarters, dimes, nickels, and pennies to purchase a pound of hamburger and a few potatoes. It was kind of fun learning about the Lord's provision.

Jessie's long walk from BIOLA to the train station wasn't thrilling, especially as she had to pass the city park where homeless winos hung out. Conscious of their watching eyes and hearing occasional whistles as she walked by accelerated her pace. Jessie's studies were curtailed with the birth of Timothy James Schlener on December 31, 1948. She became the babysitter not just to our son, but to John and Fran's son, John, in the "terrible two" stage.

Jessie was reluctant to become John's babysitter after an experience in the Bonners Ferry grocery store where she had previously worked. Somehow, John successfully tipped over a whole stack of carefully arranged canned goods onto the floor with thunderous vibrations that caught the attention of every shopper. It was Jessie's job to restack the cans.

During those years of feasting on teaching from the inspired Word of God, Jessie and I were blessed by world-renowned speakers such as Herbert Lockyer, Harry Ironside, Vance Havner, and dozens of other godly men. Veteran missionaries from nearly every country in the world kept us on the edges of our seats as they recounted their experiences about mission work during the Bible institute's annual missions conference. One valiant missionary traveled in a small sailboat from one South Pacific island to another, preaching the gospel. No private communication equipment was available in those days; no short-wave radios, computers, or cell phones.

Missionaries to China suffered opposition and persecution from those who worshipped false gods, but they seemed to meet with some success in their ministry. Missionaries referred to Africa as the Dark Continent because of the heavy influence of spiritism they encountered among the vast multitudes who never heard that Jesus

Christ, God's Son, shed His blood on the cross to pay the penalty for their sins. Many spirit worshippers tortured themselves in an attempt to somehow atone for their sins; others were cannibals, which was unimaginable to me.

India's reverence of animals—such as cows—proved another mystery. How could they worship animals? Was it possible that Hindus never enjoyed a delicious meal of roast beef and potatoes with gravy? I couldn't believe that anyone would worship an animal instead of its Creator!

Second Corinthians chapter four, verses three through five, explain the reason for the amazingly sad misconceptions held by multitudes of human beings: "Even if our gospel is veiled, it is veiled to those who are perishing. The god of this age has blinded the minds of unbelievers, so that they cannot see the light of the gospel of the glory of Christ, who is the image of God. For we do not preach ourselves, but Jesus Christ as Lord, and ourselves as your servants for Jesus' sake. For God, who said, 'Let light shine out of darkness,' made His light shine in our hearts to give us the knowledge of the glory of God in the face of Christ." (NIV Version)

Stirring, challenging messages based on the Holy Scriptures and personal interaction with veteran missionaries made Jessie and me realize that we, as Christians, were also responsible to carry the gospel message to those who had never heard. As I recall, there was little mention made regarding a need for missionaries to the Amazon River region of Brazil until we met Blake Rogers in October 1950, in Philadelphia. At that time, Jessie and I were in candidate class for the Association of Baptists for World Evangelism (ABWE) to become missionaries ourselves. Blake was on furlough from Brazil and described to prospective missionaries the pioneer work he and his family were doing in the Amazonas region. Jessie and I listened, spellbound.

Reasons for lack of response from candidates regarding the need in this region might have been that it was intensely hard to reach, and to traverse once there, the only highway was the mighty Amazon River itself. What young family wanted to spend its life in a place described by explorers and adventurers as "the green hell"? An enormous collection of snakes, bugs, spiders, termites, vampire bats and Equatorial heat, intensified by humidity from heavy rain, made the area "uncomfortable" to say the least. No hospitals existed, no supermarkets, no electricity, and no running water.

Jessie and I found ourselves under pressure even more severe than what we faced while standing in front of Pastor Walsh four years earlier. Each missionary candidate had to appear before a committee of ABWE executive officials for an oral examination. The dignified gentlemen and one lady consisted of theologians, philosophers, professors, preachers, and a foreign missionary; the group was heavily loaded with academic credentials and multiplied years of ministry.

These special people had conducted a steady stream of interviews for several days and I recall that only one member of the group was actually smiling. But the smile gave me a spark of hope that at least one person favored Jessie and me. He was a missionary back to the U.S. for furlough, and for all we knew, he might just have escaped martyrdom and was simply happy to be alive.

As we stood awaiting the first question, I was stiff and cold as a winter stone. I figured I would soon be making the rounds of employment agencies to place "situation wanted" advertisements in the local newspapers. If each board member held a copy of Jessie's and my qualifications in front of them, surely they were stumped as to what questions to ask us.

Despite our misgivings, Jessie and I learned that the ABWE board members were compassionate, humble servants of God. By God's grace and Jessie's winning smile, we made it through the interview on our feet.

The final meal at the end of 30-day missionary candidate training found most of the class uptight, less talkative, and with less appetite than usual, as we waited for phone calls from headquarters. For the entire thirty days of class, our children had been left with folks back home, and husbands and wives were housed in separate dormitory facilities. We were assigned menial work, listened to speakers each morning and evening, and learned about the operations of missions within ABWE. At any second, a phone call to each missionary would reveal our immediate futures.

At the first ring of the telephone, everyone stopped chewing. The call was answered by a retired missionary, present for that very purpose. "Sam, it's for you," he said. Sam took the phone and listened for what seemed like more than a minute. Some of us wondered if he were being given a lengthy list of reasons for why he couldn't be accepted by the mission. Sam thanked the caller, replaced the receiver gently on its hook, then threw up his hands and yelled, "Whoopee!" somewhat out of style for that setting.

"What was it, Sam?"

"I'm in, thank God!" he responded, hugging his wife who gave way to a fit of giggles.

The phone rang over and over until each of the missionaries received personal word from headquarters as to whether or not we were accepted as missionary appointees with ABWE. At long last, I heard, "Paul Schlener, this is for you."

"Brother Paul, how is your evening?" the caller asked. He took me by surprise, but I knew he wasn't asking about the kitchen fare.

"Good, thank you, but I'll enjoy it much more after this call!"

"Well Paul, I'm pleased to inform you that you and your brother John and your precious wives, Jessie and Fran, have been accepted as missionaries with ABWE, appointed to serve in the vast Amazon basin of Brazil."

I held the phone in stunned silence, wondering if there might have been some oversight in the committee's deliberation, until he asked, "Paul? Are you still there?" I stammered out a word of thanks before hanging up so I could relay the good news to Jessie.

From this unremarkable beginning sprang decades of successful missionary work in the Amazon jungles of Brazil, which thrives to this day in towns and cities up-river and down river from the Port of Two Brothers.

This story continues with the first chapter in the book Port of Two Brothers available on Internet through Amazon.com, and from ABWE Publishing, PO Box 8585, Harrisburg, PA, 71705.

The first sentence of the book says: "With ONE-WAY TICKETS, it wouldn't be easy to turn back. Our salary was small and all we had was in our suitcases. My wife Jessie and I, together with my brother John and his wife Fran, were on our way as young missionaries to what geographers call 'The Green Hell,' the jungles of Brazil bordering the mighty Amazon River.' "

****